I ONCE WAS BLIND
(1 Corinthians 6:9-19)

BUT NOW I SEE
(John 3:3-6)

MINISTER AARON WEAVER

Minister Aaron Weaver

I ONCE WAS BLIND, BUT NOW I SEE

Minister Aaron Weaver

Pearly Gates Publishing LLC
INSPIRING CHRISTIAN AUTHORS TO BE AUTHORS
Pearly Gates Publishing, LLC, Houston, Texas

I Once Was Blind, But Now I See

I Once Was Blind, But Now I See

Copyright © 2018
Minister Aaron Weaver

All Rights Reserved.
No portion of the publication may be reproduced, stored in any electronic system, or transmitted in any form or by any means (electronic, mechanical, photocopy, recording, or otherwise) without written permission from the publisher. Brief quotations may be used in literary reviews.

ISBN 13: 978-1-947445-32-1
Library of Congress Control Number: 2018951748

Scripture references are taken from the King James Version of the Holy Bible and used with permission from Zondervan via Biblegateway.com. Public Domain.

For information and bulk ordering, contact:
Pearly Gates Publishing, LLC
Angela Edwards, CEO
P.O. Box 62287
Houston, TX 77205
BestSeller@PearlyGatesPublishing.com

Minister Aaron Weaver

DEDICATION

In Loving Memory of my Precious Queen:
Verda V. Weaver.

Although the Holy Spirit was my guide as I wrote this book,
Verda was my inspiration. She often told me,
"Don't give up, Aaron. You're doing a great job!"
She was the heartbeat of my book of poetry. In fact, she lives
in every poem. She was my heart and my determination.
I asked God for the BEST wife for me, and He sent me Verda.
Her heart was pure as gold, tried by the true love of God.
She was my encouragement. She was patient.
We knew that God had put us together.
She knew how I felt without me saying a word.
We even knew each other's thoughts.
I thank God for giving me His daughter—a woman whose
first love was Him [God]. She was a prayer warrior and a
faithful, loving wife and mother. She had a heart for all
children. Her prayer was that she could one day wrap her
arms around every child in the world.
And you know what?
Sometimes I felt that Verda really did.

ACKNOWLEDGMENTS

A special thanks to Priscilla Anderson, my BFF in Texas, who confirmed and supported my move to Amite, Louisiana.

To my BFF, mighty prayer warrior, and leader over the Warfare Prayerline Ministry, thank you for your continued assistance and support in helping me get settled in Amite.

To Dareen and Michael Butler, thank you for introducing me to Pearly Gates Publishing.

To Pearly Gates Publishing and Angela Edwards, CEO, thank you for your continued support and for making my first book truly remarkable.

I would like to take this opportunity to thank all of those who kept encouraging me not to give up. I appreciate **ALL** of your support.

PREFACE

Legally Blind with Spiritual Sight

To all who read this book—which was given to me by the Holy Spirit—understand that I am legally blind. A lot of businesses and people view my condition as a liability versus an asset to them. As a man of God and low-vision individual, I am very well aware of my limitations, but I don't allow them to rule or control my life and those things I know I am able to accomplish.

Every day is a walk of faith. I **TRULY** walk by faith and not by sight. For example, when I walked to the store, it's a lot like venturing into a thick fog. My visibility may be about 20 feet away—on a *good* day. Other times, people and objects are just silhouettes, requiring me to get right up on a person (or object) to see who or what it is. Because of this eye disease called *Glaucoma*, I can only see through certain spots in my eyes. So, if you're not in that "spot", I may not see you at all. In spite of my condition, the Holy Spirit guides me. How, you ask?

God has gifted me with **Spiritual Sight**! He guides me through the natural on a daily basis, but the spiritual is what He lets me both see *and* live in. Admittedly, I felt so lost when my eyesight began to fail, but I now know that God shows me more in the spirit realm than what many others see in the natural. God has given me insight to see the heart [spirit] first so that I will not be misled by the physical anymore.

Peace to you.
~ Minister Aaron Weaver ~

INTRODUCTION

This book is designed to draw all men back to God Almighty: our first love. As men, we have strayed away from the truth of what it is to be a real man. Every man (or woman) who reads this book will see themselves in their old lifestyle and will (prayerfully) be inspired to make a change for the better.

As men in our immature state, when confronted with decision-making, we lack wisdom and knowledge when placed on the pathway of life. The result is fear, leading to doubt about our ability to lead. On many occasions, we make excuses and hide behind our pride, jobs, money, denial, and even our religious beliefs. We must "man up" and admit what we don't know. We must stop trying to look and play the part of a man when a relationship with God hasn't been established.

On the pages of this book are things I've experienced, as well as those things that God Almighty has given me—Revelation Knowledge—that I am blessed to share with you. I was instructed to write this book by a prophet of the Lord God Almighty. This book is a product of being open to receive direction from men and women of God.

You will also learn why you, your spouse, family members, children, friends, and associates act the way they do. You will discover what the causes are for sexual and child abuse, wife-beating, divorce, and mental anguish, along with why so many people are ill and what causes children to die so young. Have you ever wondered what's causing our youth to fail in life? You just may find the answer here.

Minister Aaron Weaver

With a sincere heart, I ask that women read this book as well. Why? Because they play a significant role in the lives of the men in their lives, whether it's a husband, son, boyfriend, or father, or another significant male figure.

A message to the women: I address some things concerning you as well, in hopes of helping you to become the woman God has called you to be. Be forewarned, however: Some things may not "sound nice" but know that it's the truth given in love. Please take it as a form of correction, not as an offense.

Moving forward, you will find the word **"REMEMBER"** repeated throughout this book. This is used to signify that the verse, passage, or sentence to follow is very important and that you should pay close attention to the message being relayed.

As you read, may your eyes be opened and your ears be sensitive to the very voice of God. Ask the Holy Spirit to give **YOU** Divine Revelation Knowledge. Be open to allowing the Christ in you to take His rightful place in your life.

Before we proceed, let us take a moment to reintroduce ourselves back to our Heavenly Father as we open our hearts and minds to receive what He has to say.

OPENING PRAYER

Father, in the Name of Jesus:

I ask that you open my spiritual eyes and ears, that I may receive into my life Your divine will for me and that the conviction of the Holy Spirit rest upon me as I repent and turn from the wicked ways in my life (read 2 Chronicles 7:14).

God, help me to become the man, leader, husband, father, son, or young man you have called me to be.

Also, Dear Lord, help all the women and young women who are reading this book. Deliver and set them free from the snare of the enemy (read John 3:1-7).

In Jesus' Name, we pray,

Amen.

TABLE OF CONTENTS

DEDICATION	VI
ACKNOWLEDGMENTS	VII
PREFACE	VIII
INTRODUCTION	IX
OPENING PRAYER	XI

CHAPTER 1

A RENEWED MIND 1

CHAPTER 2

THE FATHER, THE DADDY, AND THE HUSBAND 30

CHAPTER 3

DISCIPLINED 81

CHAPTER 4

PRIDE AND SELFISHNESS 92

CHAPTER 5

TRADITIONS AND HOLIDAYS 98

CHAPTER 6

THE WOMAN IN AUTHORITY 116

CHAPTER 7

SUBMISSION AND REBELLION 129

CHAPTER 8

THE YOUTH DILEMMA: PART 1 140

CHAPTER 9

THE YOUTH DILEMMA: PART 2 150

CHAPTER 10

INSIGHT, DREAMS, AND VISIONS 165

CONCLUSION 182

CLOSING PRAYER – A NEW BEGINNING FOR YOU 185

Minister Aaron Weaver

I Once Was Blind, But Now I See

CHAPTER 1

A Renewed Mind

Many men are blind to the things of God because of what they have been taught by their fathers, uncles, brothers, friends, or other prominent male figures in their lives—ones who know little to nothing themselves about being or becoming a real man. Most only know those things they have learned from the streets such as:

- ✓ Smoking
- ✓ Drinking
- ✓ Gambling
- ✓ Drug use
- ✓ Illegal hustles
- ✓ Sleeping with prostitutes or chasing anything in a skirt
- ✓ Cussing and engaging in vulgar conversations
- ✓ Pleasuring oneself with illicit behaviors to include:
    - o Viewing pornographic books, videos, and websites
- ✓ Teaching our young boys and men to abuse, lie, and cheat on their wives or girlfriends

NOTE: That is not the role model of a **REAL** man.

As a society, we have been told that a man is not supposed to cry. However, when a man cries, it allows the release of disappointment and hurt that dwells deep within his soul. Crying is a defense for grief and many illnesses, but if you hold it in, it can kill you—especially if you have an unforgiving heart!

How can you expect God to hear your prayers or release His blessings to you while you're bathing in bitterness?

I Once Was Blind, But Now I See

REMEMBER: Don't let unforgiveness keep you from entering into the Kingdom of God!

When a man has taught any of the behaviors above, he displays a spirit of immaturity and ignorance. In response, doors are open for both familiar and unfamiliar spirits to come forth and operate in not only his life but the lives of others as well. This is called a "spoken curse" or "transference of spirits." The curse is almost as bad as death itself, and that curse is called "Failure."

Here's the truth of the matter: We just taught our sons and other young men how to fail at something that's imperative…how to become a mature man **AND** man of God! Our young men must learn how to have respect for themselves and everyone else.

Consider the man who "shacks up" with a woman – the one with no intentions of making her his bride. The only real benefit is the security of having himself a "piece" at home, all while trying to fulfill his lustful appetite. "Shacking up" frees him from his sense of responsibility and commitment to himself, the woman, and **GOD**. This type of relationship will lead him into a perpetual state of immaturity. When a man functions in this manner, there is no genuine respect for the woman…or himself. If there is enough love to live together, then love enough to get married!

REMEMBER: Your body lacks intelligence. It's your brain that will sometimes make decisions on how you feel, think, or see things. This is why we must be led by the Spirit of God to make the correct choices. *"He who desires wisdom, let him ask."* (Read James 1:5-6; Proverbs 3:5-7.)

Gentlemen, for many years, we have operated with ignorance, foolishness, and lack of training and wise counsel in the development into manhood. Why? Because we have refused to seek **THE ONE** who will set us on the right path: ***GOD***. He is **THE ONE** who gives us wisdom and wise counsel through His Word, as well as our following the guidance of the Holy Spirit. However, at some point in our lives, we have all but eliminated God out of the equation of our manhood.

How many times have you gone out drinking with your friends or by yourself and have had the following conversation the next day?

*"Man, I was so messed up, I didn't even know where I was or what I was doing! Oh, but it felt **SO** good! I was **SO** high, I messed around with my wife's sister and got some from her! That was some good stuff! Maybe she'll let me tap that again!"*

Those words may sound funny to you and your friends at first, but there is nothing humorous about adultery, fornication, or sexual and physical abuse. Actually, that is a path Satan has laid out for us and far too often, we have fallen into his trap. When it happens, we are operating in lack of wisdom, knowledge, and understanding concerning the will, Word, and way of God for our lives as men.

REMEMBER: If you are a Christian and operating in that manner, you are now a carnal-minded Christian.

- Romans 8:5 – *"For they that are after the flesh, mind the things of the flesh; and those that are after the Spirit mind the things of the Spirit."*
- Romans 8:7 – *"Because the carnal mind is enmity [opposed] against God..."* Now, go and read Romans 8:8-9 for yourself.

REMEMBER: The wages of sin is death, but the gift of God is eternal life. *"Be not wise in thy own eyes: Fear the Lord and depart from evil"* (Proverbs 3:7).

Taking a Stand

As men, it's time we relinquish Satan's control of the keys to our lives, our marriages, our families, our finances, and even the dreams and visions we have of different businesses and inventions we've had but never made an effort to follow through on them.

Why is that so? Is it because of the spirit of fear, procrastination, or fear of success? We must take a stand and recover all that the enemy has stolen from us! We must regain control!

As parents, one of the first things we must do is give our children back to God so that He may train them in the areas where we have fallen short.

REMEMBER: We are crippling them by doing everything for them.

Don't try to live your children's lives.

Don't overwhelm them by giving them what you didn't have or receive from your parents.

Don't try to run, rule, or operate your life, home, or marriage the way your parents ran theirs.

Listen: Your children are not here to live out your dreams or fulfill your purpose. They are meant to travel down the path that God has designed just for them.

God Almighty loves us; not our sins. He gave us life and a will to choose whether to serve Him and live (everlasting life) OR reject Him and die (eternal separation from God) by being cast into the Lake of Fire with Satan, the fallen angels, the beast, and all others who oppose God.

REMEMBER: Our bodies are temples of the Holy Spirit. We must give an account of everything we've done in and with His temple.

REMEMBER: God gave you life. He placed Himself in mankind from the beginning (see Genesis 2:7).

As you read the next passage of scripture, put your name in the place of "My son."

Proverbs 3:1-2

"My son, forget not my law, but let thy heart keep My commandments. For length of days, and long life, and peace shall thy add to thee."

God is placing those words in your heart just from reading them. Don't take them for granted. He loves you and wants to set you free.

Our sons and daughters should be treated like royalty. They are not to be tarnished by you or any other in any way under any circumstance. God has trusted us and placed them in our care. If we abuse them, inevitably, we will answer to God. You won't be able to justify your actions or your words (see Matthew 12:36-37).

A Fine-Tuned Marriage

> **REMEMBER:** With every temptation,
> God has made way for us to escape.

Men, treat your wife like a precious ruby—a stone so valuable, it's priceless. She should be polished on a daily basis to the utmost, as fine silver. She should be honored, respected, and treated like your "Precious Queen" every day.

Your marriage is likened to a high-performance jet: Your choice of fuel will determine how well it will fly. Without proper maintenance, it will lose altitude and crash!

Maybe your marriage is more like a fine automobile. It requires both a positive and negative post to start the car. In that way, you and your wife must be opposite in some ways to make the marriage work. Still, both of you are attached to the battery (the battery is the Word of God). If either of you disconnects, the marriage cannot ignite. The voltage coming from the battery (the Word) is the anointing. Every time you draw from the battery, you receive a fresh anointing. If the battery dies (the Word in you), then there is no anointing in the marriage, leaving you stuck in the wilderness because of sin.

We are new creatures in Christ. Old things are passed away; behold, all things become new. Don't disconnect yourself from JESUS, the power in our lives!

Encounters of the Ungodly Kind

Let's briefly touch on perverted spirits. At this moment, what the Holy Spirit is saying to me is this:

"STOP calling them 'gay'; they just have a homosexual or lesbian spirit attached to them."

REMEMBER: Whenever we call them by that name, we are giving those spirits authority to operate in their lives. Scripture tells us there are life and death in the power of the tongue (see Proverbs 18:21). For many years, we have labeled the person instead of addressing the spirit.

I'm about to get real raw here...

God, Jesus, and the Holy Spirit did not "make" anyone gay or lesbian. God made man and then made a woman to help him and to fulfill his needs (see Genesis 1:27).

When the **CHOICE** is made to sleep with a same-sex partner, the message that's being conveyed is that the participant knows more than God and that God didn't know what He was doing. The **CHOICE** was made to live that way (see Proverbs 3:5-7; 16:25). If the **CHOICE** is made to not repent and accept Jesus as your personal Savior (see John 3:16; Romans 5:8), then know that you are essentially ready to give up eternal life with Jesus for a few years of pleasure in the flesh. Are you willing to let the corruption of Satan guide you down the path to Hell into the eternal Lake of Fire—a place prepared especially for him and his fallen angels?

When we encounter a man or woman who's under the influence of a gay or lesbian spirit, we must stand boldly and let them know that they are under the control of a perverted spirit. But don't stop there! We must also tell them that Jesus can set them free. In doing so, we are supplying them with wisdom and knowledge so that they can get an understanding and make an educated decision—not one made because of what they think they are or because they believe they were born that way or because of what someone told them they were or because of what happened to them as a child, in prison, or from an unfortunate encounter with a family member. There are even those who were forced into performing same-sex acts against their will who have succumbed to that lifestyle.

There's good news, though! Many people have been set free from that immoral act! God doesn't hate them; He hates sin.

We must tell them that God loves them, we love them, and that this way of living is not right. It's no different than telling a pervert, wife-beater, thief, rapist, drunk driver, or anyone else who's doing something wrong. What they are doing is not right, and there are severe consequences behind the **CHOICES** they make (see 1 Corinthians 6:9-10; Romans 10:9-10).

Every decision we make has either a good **OR** bad outcome. To make it plain: Those who choose to commit adultery or fornication may be facing the same outcome as someone in a homosexual relationship if they choose not to repent and keep sleeping around. There is no such thing (in the will of God) as "common-law marriage" or "palimony."

REMEMBER: God does **NOT** reward unrepentant sinners. (Read Proverbs 3:5-6; John 4:16-18.)

Politicians—mayors, governors, and lawmakers in Washington—have removed good morals and the righteousness of God's will, His Word, and His way. Slowly, they are trying to dismantle the way God pre-destined for us to live so that they can "control" us with political slavery. The worst part of this is that we have permitted the "takeover" by not taking a stand against the leaders of the United States of America. In our silence, we have all but compromised with our political leaders (see 2 Chronicles 7:14). We must pray that their heart of stone that dwells within them be destroyed, and let it be replaced with a spirit of love and compassion for the people (see Ezekiel 36:26).

Passiveness and Making the Right Decision

Gentlemen, you must have a renewed mind when it comes to making the right decision or taking your rightful place.

Let's start with the basics.

I Once Was Blind, But Now I See

Do you ask your wife or significant other to go out on dates **OR** do she have to ask you to take them somewhere all or most of the time? For some, this may be a new frontier for you. If so, let's start "small" by introducing the idea something like this:

*"Sweetheart [insert your love's nickname here], let's go to a movie tonight or something else special. Is there anywhere, in particular, **YOU** would like to go this weekend?"*

Making plans to do something is very important in any relationship—especially marriage. Whenever you make a decision involving finances or family, be sure to include her in the decision-making process. By doing so, you are letting her know how important she is and how much you value her input. Most importantly, it is reflective of both of you being on one accord. By choosing not to include her, you make your home dysfunctional (use discretion when hosting a surprise party, anniversary celebration, or another momentous event in your lives).

As a man, if you choose not to take your rightful place, you are operating under an Ahab spirit (a passive spirit) and give authority and leadership to the wife (or girlfriend).

REMEMBER: A man without a backbone makes the home dysfunctional.

For about 12 years, I made a fool out of myself by operating under the Ahab spirit, but God saw me through it. I came out victorious! He delivered me as Jesus set me free!

If you're involved in a relationship wherein you are functioning as an Ahab, remove yourself from the home and get out of that relationship because the situation will continue to pull you down. If she's living with you, then she needs to get her own place or move in with family or friends.

Take it from a veteran in this "game": It's not worth losing out on God's blessings.

Another area where I have had to renew my mind is this: Men, please don't trade sex for your manhood. Respect yourself and your honor as a man. If you're married, take your rightful place as the husband and leader so that you can fully operate under your God-given authority.

(Now I know why I was often told, *"No, Aaron. You're a nice guy. I like you, but only as a friend."*)

Gentleman, you were not called to be a stay-home dad (this is also a sign of an Ahab spirit). I'm just going to put it out there: If this is what you have chosen to do while your wife has taken on the task of carrying the household, then you had no business getting married. This does not include a man who has a home-based business, is bed-stricken, or physically/mentally unable to work. Think about this: When you get older, how can you draw Social Security benefits if you never held a job?

A man who follows a pattern of staying home and letting a woman take care of him likely had, at some point in his life, a relationship that inflicted on him a spirit of intimidation or low self-esteem. Absent was the guidance needed on what his role as a man or husband is supposed to be. Perhaps he was spoiled or "babied"—not just as a child, but also as a grown man. Maybe he is merely one of those men who didn't want to listen.

When a man becomes of age, he should take care of himself and not run to mommy, daddy, or his significant other all the time for money, a place to stay, or as a way out of situations he placed himself into.

Let me ask: Do you think it's a safe and comfortable place to not mature into manhood? You can be honest here. Only you and God know the **TRUTH** about you.

Moving along…

Maybe you're afraid of being alone or are in the relationship just for the sex. If you choose to marry because she is financially secure or just for the sexual benefits, then you're operating under a spirit of witchcraft by using the spirits of deception and manipulation. If you're already in this dilemma, God is pressing you at this moment to take your rightful place.

If you are a man seeking work and have to secure a position, stop trying to find one on your own. Each day, seek God **FIRST**. Stay before Him in prayer and listen to His voice. On your own, you could be looking too hard and possibly miss out on the job God has just for you.

The Controller

The Jezebel spirit typically attaches itself to women; however, it can affect men as well. When it connects to a man, he can become overbearing. He will find himself using harsh language, always yelling and practicing other aggressive behaviors such as fighting and demanding sex. These are acts of a controlling spirit. Some men won't allow their wife or girlfriend to leave the house or go anywhere without him. They won't permit visitors or casual chatter on the phone. Because of this, many women are prisoners in their own home. The man makes the woman feel useless and as if no one else would want her but him. The bondage of low self-esteem is at play.

There was a lot I needed to learn about the Jezebel spirit. What did God do? He sent me my wife, Verda. However, before Verda became my wife, God used her to open my eyes to this spirit and helped me to stay focused on who I was in Christ. She knew more about the spirit than I did because, at one point in her life, she operated under the influence of the Jezebel spirit for a long time. God could not put me in her life as a leader and husband until I was ready.

Did I know everything I needed to before we married?

No! Neither one of us knew everything.

REMEMBER: Everyone must seek God daily and be open to receive His wise counsel.

Trial and Error

Many women have become so independent today and say that it's hard for them to find a man who will step up to the plate and take his rightful place as a man, father, and husband.

Ladies, that is your first mistake.

I Once Was Blind, But Now I See

Don't judge or condemn the man. It just may be that you keep picking the wrong type of man…and he keeps choosing the wrong woman! Both of you must renew your mind daily and let God guide you in your decision-making. When you don't, you are rapidly becoming a repeat offender.

If you see that the relationship is following the same pattern as ones before, back up and reevaluate the relationship immediately. If you're smart, you will find out all of this before you jump into the bed. Just because he's a man, cute, fine, or because he tells you all the right things does **NOT** make him "the one for you."

REMEMBER: Ask him a lot of questions. Ask about his mother, father, sister, brother, other family members, and even his friends (in other words, **BE NOSY**).

Gentlemen, the same thing applies to you. Ask a lot of questions. Let the Holy Spirit guide you. Use the head on your shoulders to make decisions; not the one between your legs or what's between her thighs.

REMEMBER: Stop adding fuel to the fire for both of you to become even MORE dysfunctional! Both of you have issues (that's life), but without GOD, they will never be resolved.

About the Children

Do **NOT** get married or stay involved in a dysfunctional relationship just because of the children. If there's no genuine love between the two of you, don't subject yourselves or the children to that dysfunctional and abusive lifestyle.

BUT DO NOT — I repeat — **DO NOT NEGLECT YOUR RESPONSIBILITIES AS A FATHER.** Build a relationship with God and your child(ren). Put your trust in God. Seek Him first — not man or the world's "system."

Ladies, do not sell your body or freely give it to a man just to make a dollar. Don't use your "money-maker" (as the world calls it) to take care of yourself and your children. Seek God and trust Him, and He will see you through (read Matthew 6:33).

Men, if you had children before you married, be sure to give them your last name. Your name is the foundation for their future. It also gives them a man or person to identify themselves with and can help them find other family members years down the line.

Men, if you're married and have committed adultery that resulted in children outside of the marriage, you have just placed your son/daughter on "Failure Road." You deposited into an unauthorized account, and now, your account with your children has been closed because of NSF fees (No Support from the Father). I ask: What kind of withdrawal can you make from this type of situation? If you are guilty, ask for God's forgiveness, repent, and ask God to have mercy on you, the other woman, and the children. Pray in earnest that the curse stops with **YOU** — in Jesus' Name.

Character Development

One way to describe maturity is: One who uses wisdom when making a decision; one who takes or gives wise counsel.

Maturity isn't something you fall into or get when you turn 18 or 21 years old. This character of your manhood must be developed. It requires a lot of stripping away by God of the things in your life to get you to the level He has called you to be.

REMEMBER: There is no specific age that God develops a man into manhood.

Look, let's get down to the bare facts. A woman doesn't need just a good, stiff one in bed. She also needs a man who will provide security in her life and hold her at night to comfort her without sex all the time. She needs a man she can look up to as a father (or father's image).

Inside every woman is a little girl waiting to be released. At the same time, she still needs to be a woman. When the time comes to be a little girl, that's when she wants the comfort of a father. She desires to be held by you and assured that everything will be alright. Sometimes, she's not even aware of it herself. All she knows is that something is missing — and it needs to come from **YOU**. That is the fatherly-love she's searching for. Whether she had a father in her home when she was growing up or not, she now needs that hug and sincere expression of security from **YOU**. Give her what she needs by showing her intimacy — not just sex all the time because if that's what you're doing, you're not supplying her needs. The truth of the matter is that you're only getting from her what you want.

REMEMBER: You, as the husband, must learn from God how to operate as the prophet, priest, king, pastor, and counselor of your home.

It's time-out for the dumb stuff. It's past time to put all the myths about what women want and need behind you, along with all that mess you have been taught from the streets about what a 'real man' is.

Gentleman, the same thing applies to your sons. They also need to be shown love and what love is. If you don't show them love, they won't know how to treat their girlfriend and wife.

Another thing the Holy Spirit revealed to me is that boys grow up to be a man, but every man is not mature; girls grow up to be a woman, but every woman is not a lady.

Think about this: Why take lessons from a loser? If your family member or friend has had a number of failed relationships of marriages, let's face it: Something was wrong!

What could the problem be? Well...

- Did they really love each other?
- Were they given wise counsel?
- Was God the center of their lives?
- Was money the reason?
- Was Jesus the Ruler and Head of the marriage?
- Did they get married because of the sex?
- Was she pregnant?
- Was it a "shotgun" wedding?

- Did they marry so that the child(ren) could have a two-parent household?
- Maybe they were together for so long, they felt it was time to get married!

Someone reading this may have gotten married out of love, but you knew that he/she was not the right person for you before you said: *"I do."* You went into the marriage thinking the other party would change or that you could change them. Never enter a relationship or marriage thinking you can change the other person or that time will effect change. You can't change them **OR** yourself; God and **ONLY GOD** can do the changing, and He will do it in both of you…if you welcome Him in.

REMEMBER: Your marriage is the standard in which God has commanded for you to live.

If you choose to mimic your relatives, friends, television and movie stars, singers, and athletes (to name a few), then that's just as bad.

The men of today that choose to let God govern their lives are still in training. God is training them through His Word in all aspects of life: maturity, leadership, obedience, and discipline. Why is there ongoing training? So that the men of God will be equipped to train other men!

Gentlemen, we will **NEVER** reach that 100% mark because growth and maturity have no end. Ask yourself these questions:

➤ How many men have sat down with you and given you wise counsel?
➤ How many have given you positive direction for your life by using the Word of God and not the deceptive ways of the world?
➤ How can you instruct another to be a man, unless you have taken lessons or been given direction from the One who made you: God?

REMEMBER: We must use the Holy Bible as a roadmap for us to live and be trained under the power of the **ALMIGHTY GOD** through the **HOLY SPIRIT**.

The "Highway to Manhood" is never-ending. It is a daily walk with God with a well-established prayer life, constant study of His Word, and followed up by obedience and a teachable spirit which flows from a humble heart.

Your life is like a rollercoaster — full of ups and downs, curves and loops. It doesn't matter if you're married or not; decision-making is the balance beam of life. If you go a little too far to the left or right, you fall off the narrow path.

In the Bible story of Peter, as long as he kept his eyes on Christ, he was able to literally walk on water. As soon as he took his eyes off Jesus and began to focus on the storm (or the issues of life), he immediately began to sink.

REMEMBER: The man who walks in the will of God goes through the issues of life with the assurance that God will be with him. God will never leave you nor forsake you.

Anyone who goes through life without Jesus as their Savior is on a path of destruction and headed to Hell with their eyes wide open. Why is that so? Because they have placed their trust in man, the things of this world, their good deeds, idols, zodiac signs, the earthly elements and stars, as well as their family or religious traditions, money, or they lean on their own understanding (doing things their way).

"The heart of the wise teaches his mouth and added learning to his lips" (Proverbs 16:23).

"There is a way that seems right unto a man, but the end thereof is the ways of death" (Proverbs 16:25).

REMEMBER: JESUS is the only One who was and is the Word. He came from Heaven, was born of a virgin, performed many miracles, died on the cross at Calvary, rose from the dead, left the Holy Spirit with us, went back to Heaven, and is now sitting at the right-hand side of our Father, the **LORD GOD ALMIGHTY**, interceding for all of us. Jesus is coming back for His people. There is no other name in Heaven, on the earth, or in the universe that saved man from sin and redeemed him [man] back to God.

Pastors, Step UP!

How many of you have heard the following statement before?

"If you're looking for a good man or woman, go to church."

Pastors, this one's for you! The women and young ladies are your "daughters," and the men and young men are your "sons." It is your responsibility to protect them. It is also the responsibility of the church leaders to protect and guide them as well.

It's not about just going to Sunday school. It's not about one's position in the church, either. Satan goes around like a roaring lion, especially in the church! After all, it's his never-ending supply of food. Sadly, many pastors are still permitting this atrocity to continue in their churches. Some pastors, church leaders, and members blatantly turn their heads away from the obvious presence of the enemy.

Pastors, ask yourself: *"Am I an Ahab? Are there witches, warlocks, and Jezebel spirits that have taken control of my church?"* If so, get yourself and your church together **NOW** — or take a seat. If you don't put a stop to the unruly spirits, God **WILL** hold you accountable.

REMEMBER: Where much is given, much is required. Never forget you are your brother's and sister's keeper. Just because they are in the church doesn't mean they're saved, and just because they're saved, they still need to be delivered.

The church is not a quick-fix hospital, even though there are many people sick (with sin) who attend. Many are in the congregation, with some of them being leaders. Among the list of the worst things that can happen is that some of them could become a pastor. We all have been wounded along life's journey. Sheep will injure sheep. Goats will continue to kick up confusion. The wolves, however, will devour you. Don't run from the hurt. Take a stand and bring it to the Lord. We can't grow without going through the storms of life.

The church must be trained to become mature men and women of God so that they can teach the children how to conduct themselves. They learn responsibility by working and studying in school and their bibles.

REMEMBER: Bring all your cares before the Lord in prayer that He may give you [pastors and men] a strategy or plan to help in developing the children of God.

Clean It Up Before It's Too Late!

Men of God, as you seek Him for guidance when you're training the sons and daughters of the church, help the mother or sister (if either needs your support) by giving them wise counsel in this area. Remember to keep God first. Teach the children how to apply the Word as well as how to pray. You must be an example and not have a woman living with you or vice-versa if she is not your wife. Stop cussing and rid your home of the dirty books, videos, pornographic websites and phone numbers, and magazines. Humble yourself and keep your tongue in the presence of your children and others.

Ladies, that applies to you, too!

"Set a watch, O Lord, before my mouth…"
(Psalm 141:3)

"There's death and life in the power of the tongue."
(Proverbs 18:21)

REMEMBER: God gave you life and the chance for eternal life through Jesus Christ. He woke you up this morning. With the very first sin you committed, you could have died instantly, for the wages of sin is death. God's grace saved us and His mercy keeps us, for his mercy endures forever.

Man of God, He has called you to be the leader; the head. He has given you the chance to finish where Adam fell short (see Genesis 1:28).

It's unfortunate that today, many homes lack the leadership of a father to help the children become the men and women of God they are called to be. We must first seek the Kingdom of God by gaining wisdom, for fear of the Lord is the beginning of wisdom.

"Set not your treasures on this earth..." (read Matthew 6:19-23).

Don't just seek after the things of this world or you may be lured into its grasp and operate in its system. The "world's" system includes some of the following:

- Compulsive lying
- Theft
- Robbery
- Murder
- Excessive drinking
- Drug addiction
- Rape
- Womanizing
- Adultery
- Prostitution (including call-girl and escort services)

- Posing nude in magazines and videos
- The relentless pursuit of money and fame
- Practicing black or white magic (both are evil)
- Idolatry (anything or anybody put before God is called idolatry and will lead you into a life of misery, loneliness, and death)

"Be not deceived: neither fornicators, nor idolaters, nor adulterers, nor effeminate [womanish, unmanly], nor abusers of themselves with mankind. Nor thieves, nor covetous, nor drunkards, nor revilers, nor extortionists, shall inherit the kingdom of God" (read more at 1 Corinthians 6:9-19).

Remember I said earlier that if you don't repent, you will become those things (in other words, those spirits will have a great influence over the decisions you make). Eventually, they will take over your life. Instead of you being in control of them, they will control you. However, if you seek the things of God, you will reap a harvest of blessing, such as long life on this earth, peace, joy, divine favor, respect, self-control, and more (see Matthew 12:33-37; Proverbs 3:1-4; 1 Corinthians 12:8-10; Galatians 5:22-26).

Just remember this: You must renew your mind to the things of God. Why? Because if you don't, you will never really experience what it is to be born again or know what the Kingdom of God is (see John 3:2-6).

REMEMBER: Your purpose on this earth is to praise God. In honoring and serving Him, He will guide you in the way that you should go (read Psalm 23; Proverbs 3:1-12; Proverbs 16:9).

The Conflict

The Word of God says that Satan comes to kill, steal, and destroy; however, he can only do those things when we let him in through the things we think, say, and do. In other words, he enters through our heart, which is our mind, will, emotions, and intellect. When this happens, we leave the doors and windows wide open for the following to take place in our lives:

1. We can be robbed of our joy, peace, purpose, and even identity. You may choose to live a perverted lifestyle, which is a double-minded spirit that is accompanied by a spirit of confusion.
2. The enemy comes to kill your dreams of success by putting a negative word or negative-speaking person in our life. That person's purpose is to discourage you. Anything you decide to do to bring forth your potential, he will send someone (sometimes your spouse, children, family members, or closest friends) or do whatever he can to stop it from coming to pass. He will also use the spirit of procrastination and bombard you with low self-esteem.
3. When a tragic event occurs (such as the loss of a loved one or pet), you are left feeling abandoned and that everyone or everything you love is going to leave you or die. Stop Satan before he gets a stronghold on your life. Seek God first, stay in His Word, and pray. Remember always that God will never leave you or forsake you.
4. Some of you are unwilling to fall in love because fear has a grip on you. In response, you turn to drugs and alcohol. You become disrespectful, rude, and violent. No one can talk to you or tell you anything positive. You

become depressed and possibly even suicidal. You need to talk to your earthly father, but he's nowhere to be found. What makes it worse is that some have no idea who their birth father is! You lash out at anyone desiring to show you love.

REMEMBER: Don't allow the enemy to steal your **JOY!**

Smokescreen

Many people idolize the lives of famous people. They imitate their "idol's" lifestyle and desire to live and be like them. What they are doing is searching for an identity. Here's the wake-up call: No matter who they choose to admire, they will never magically transform into them.

It's just a smokescreen.

Some young men join a gang. That union makes them feel like a member of a family, they have a place where they belong, and are encamped about by people they feel understands them. Interestingly enough, the others in the gang are in the same boat! Hurting people hurt people! The blind cannot lead the blind (in the things of God)! They are in no position to help someone else when they can't even help themselves.

My words of encouragement here are these: Be dead to that life and be alive in Christ! Let **HIM** [Jesus] be your Savior!

Satan desires to destroy every good thing about you, as well as every good thought you have about those you love and those who love you. Satan will use your emotional state of unforgiveness, vengeance, and abandonment against you to hurt others, and he will keep it up until he destroys you by death by someone else's hands or even your own.

Suicide is an attack of the enemy. Don't take your own life. Don't give him the victory! Suicide is a selfish spirit that rides shotgun with the spirit of low self-esteem. That selfish spirit will leave people crying out in pain, saying things such as:

- "I can't live without him."
- "I can't live without her."
- "I don't want to be alone anymore."
- "Let me die with my child, mother, or father."
- "I tried to kill myself because he/she doesn't love me anymore."
- "Everything I loved is dead."
- "I have nothing to live for anymore."
- "Nobody loves me; maybe they'll miss me when I'm dead."

They are all just smoke screens. I have gone through many of those afflictions. Today, I can profess loudly:

"I ONCE WAS BLIND, BUT NOW I SEE!"

I Once Was Blind, But Now I See

A Prayer of Maturity

My Heavenly Father,

Forgive me for all my sins and let not the iniquities of all my ancestors come up against me, my family, and their seeds.

Father, renew my mind and give me the wisdom to become the mature man of God you have called me to be. Let mercy and discretion guide me as your wisdom and truth teach me.

I repent this day for my immature ways and accept Jesus as my Lord and personal Savior.

Thank you, Father, that today, in the Name of Jesus, I am free!

Amen.

CHAPTER 2

THE FATHER, THE DADDY, AND THE HUSBAND

As men, we must come to know God in the fullness of His holiness; as Jehovah, our Covenant Redeemer (see Exodus 6:3-4). God is the Father of all creation. He is the founder and creator of Heaven and earth (Genesis 1:1). He is our Father, our LORD, our Master, and the Overseer of our lives. We must have a personal and intimate relationship with Him. *"Thou shall have no other god before Me"* (Exodus 20:3).

In Exodus 3:6-9, the word "am" is italicized. It was not part of the original language; it was added for better reading. Remove the word "am" and read the passage of scripture, then move along to verse fourteen. In that verse, God makes is personal. In verse 15, He makes it a little clearer when He says, *"Moreover,"* meaning beyond what has been stated.

"God said moreover unto Moses, thus shall thou say unto the children of Israel, the LORD God of your fathers, the God of Abraham, the God of Isaac, and the God of Jacob has sent me unto you. This is My name forever, and this is my memorial unto all generations" (Exodus 3:15).

In Exodus 6:3, Abraham, Isaac, and Jacob referred to God as "God Almighty," not as "Jehovah," their 'Covenant Redeemer.'

This is how God described Himself to me: *"I AM Alpha and Omega; the Beginning and the End. I AM the First and the Last. I will go before you, and I will guard your back. I AM the North and the South. I AM up high, but I see all things below. I AM the East and the West. I have no beginning or end. I AM Untouchable!"*

A Man's Role

As men, there are a lot of roles we play in our lives. It is our God-given nature to be leaders and providers.

1. It is during the first stage when our character and integrity are developed, maturity is taught, and wisdom is born.
2. Then, there is the role of a husband, in which we become responsible for the life of another person: our wife. In this stage of our maturity, we must protect, cherish, love, respect, comfort, and provide for her. We must give her shelter and always do our best to keep her in peaceful and comfortable surroundings. We must continuously strive to enhance both her inner and out beauty.
3. As the father, we are the key element in the making of a family. The true meaning of God's love should be shown, and the very image of God implemented. Remember: God will never leave you or forsake you, so this attribute should also be in the earthly father as it relates to his family. God has a personal relationship with His children, so we should have one with ours. It doesn't matter if you're married, divorced, or single; your child still needs to be able to connect with you. We are responsible for the lives and welfare of our wife and children. The decisions we make are crucial to the spiritual, physical, financial, and emotional outcome of the family.
4. The daddy is responsible for the structure and upbringing of the children, as well as the development of their lifestyle and future. He is the counselor of the

family and future generations, as he gives all of them words of wisdom.

We must be aware of everything that can affect our family now and in the times to come. We cannot absorb all the filth around us and expect to function in our respective positions. Before we can perform in our role as a man, we must first seek God for wisdom and guidance so that we can teach today's man and prepare them to teach the men of tomorrow. Learn the difference between them and how to operate in each one. As you are learning, reflect on how those differences can affect our families and us (read Proverbs 18:15-16,22).

There's an old saying that goes, *"A man may work from sun to sun, but a woman's work is never done."* Well, I must say that in my opinion, that is not 100% accurate. Whether man or woman, if they feel they must always have something to do, that is unwise. If this is you, then your life is out of balance.

REMEMBER: There's a season and a place for everything.

Don't work yourself to the point that there is no time to enjoy the fruit of your labor or to rest in God. Tradition will tell you that God worked six days and rested on the seventh. Read Genesis 1:6-31; 2:1-3 again. According to the Word, God completed His work on the seventh day, and **THEN** He rested. Everything God created He fellowshipped with and gave it a purpose—and that includes **YOU!**

Train a Child Up in the Ways of the LORD

Before you have sex with your wife…long before conception and birth take place, as parents, we should ask the Lord to reveal what gifts He has placed within the child. We should then prophesy (speak over; call forth) what the Lord God Almighty would have you name that child as well as their purpose. Pray that their gifts be used to serve Him [God] from whom they came.

PLEASE don't give your child some off-the-wall, meaningless name! Before you name your child, make sure you find out the meaning **FIRST** because what you call them is what they just may become. That child may begin to perform like "it," talk like "it," and maybe even walk like "it" — especially those nicknames!

REMEMBER: The name you give your child is just like a label.

If you name your child after a relative or friend, make sure you are fully aware of what kind of person he or she is (or was), including the type of lifestyle they live (or lived). If you have children out of wedlock, this should be prioritized all the more.

Parents, bind up all those things that are not of God that you see operating in our life (those generational curses and familiar evil spirits within your family's history). Those things that you call "hereditary," such as a drug addict, wife-beater, child molester, alcoholic, fornicator, adulterer, rebellious attitude, disobedience, heart problems, eye disease, divorce, etc. are all related to the stronghold called "Abuse."

Whatever you do, ensure your children have a childhood. Don't allow them to grow up too fast. If your child is gifted (i.e., they are only five years old with the IQ of a 12-year-old), he or she is still a **CHILD**. Support and enhance their gift but let them be a child. I have seen far too many children *AND* adults with a very high IQ and little common sense. Be sure to train them in the Word of God as well as their academic ability.

Anyone can make a dollar, but not everyone knows how to invest or spend it wisely. So, **PLEASE**—in the Name of **JESUS**—do not invest or allow your children to invest in anything that strips them from their morals or the will of God such as nightclubs, casinos, sex phone calls, vulgar music, violent video games, or illicit movies. The Word of God asks, *"What does it profit a man to gain the world and lose his soul?"*

REMEMBER: God will hold you responsible for your children's sins until they reach the age of twelve (considered the age of accountability).

From that point forward, they are held accountable for their own sins. Still, we must realize there is no way to watch them 24 hours, seven days a week. Their interests will change just as sure as the sun will rise. They will become interested in the opposite sex. There will be dances, proms, football, baseball, and basketball games, and so much more in their young lives. We must trust God, as well as the spiritual and moral training we have given them. When they reach the age of accountability and beyond, we need to pray more on a daily basis for their lives and salvation. We can't protect our children from everything; neither can we change the world by using the world's system. We must plant and speak the Word and be a partaker (a doer) of the Word of God. While we can't protect them from everything, we can and should pray on their behalf for all things. Children must learn how to put God first in their lives, and we must lead by example. We are not to compromise with them when it comes to their moral conduct.

> **REMEMBER:** Don't compromise with the devil or your children's soul.

Examine yourself. What foundation have you laid out for your children? Can you answer "yes" to even **ONE** of the following questions?

- Are you teaching them how to lie, cheat, and steal?
- Are you teaching them how to get something for nothing?
- Are you telling them how to manipulate people to get what they want?
- Are you a parent who lets your children put their hands on you and hurt you?
- Are you one of those parents who cuss and let your children cuss at you or in your presence?
- Are you one of those parents who lets your children fight with their sibling and you laugh when one makes the other cry?
- Do you permit them to question your decisions?
- Are you letting your daughter's boyfriend or your son's girlfriend move into your home?
- Are you telling them that it's okay to shack up or have a baby out of wedlock?

- Are you encouraging them to live off the system by telling them to get on welfare?
- Are you encouraging sex by telling them to make sure they use protection or some other form of birth control?
- Are you telling them it's okay to murder out of vengeance?
- Are you telling them it's okay to get an abortion?

If you replied "yes" to any one of those questions, you have already compromised your morals and respect for yourself, your children, future generations, and your home. With unwise counsel like that, it's easy to see why today's generation is out of control! Don't pass this curse down to them.

How about some more instances to consider?

- Do you accept when your son or daughter brings home their same-sex partner to spend the night?
- Do you let them kiss in your presence or home?
- Do you allow them to perform their perverted sex acts there as well?

I repeat: **DO NOT** compromise with the devil. Those things are not acceptable to God and should not be accepted by you.

One thing that has become commonplace is how some parents agree with their children shacking up before getting married. God said *"NO!"*, and you should, too. This also applies to you allowing them to use illegal drugs or getting drunk in your home with their friends or worse, **YOU!**

Far too many people believe the lies that say, *"This is MY body!"* or *"I'm grown. I can do what I want!"* Reality check! The **ONLY** people who are grown are those who are **DEAD**. They are the ones who cannot grow anymore. We have a spirit that lives in a body that God lets us use.

> **REMEMBER:** God will hold you accountable for everything you do to and in His temple. STOP compromising with these spirits!

How about an example?

If someone lets you use their car and you never clean, put oil or gas in it, or possibly wreck the car and won't help with the repairs, you have abused that which wasn't yours. You are left to deal with the consequences of your actions (or lack of).

It's imperative you acknowledge unholy spirits that are operating in your children's lives. When those spirits show up, give them the boot by praying over your children. Don't let them defile your home! When you allow your children to do whatever they want, or you give them everything they ask for, you are not teaching them responsibility or discipline. If you cave in at the mere sound of a temper tantrum and let them have their way, you are not showing them love. All that it proves is that you don't have the backbone to stand up and do what's right…or maybe you were never taught discipline and do not know how to address it head-on.

Please stop trying to buy your children's love.

Please stop trying to be their best friend. You are their parent. Don't cross that line. They may not favor the parent/child relationship, but let me ask this: Would you rather have God correct both of you?

Whether you've done your part as a parent or not, the time comes when you have to give your children to God. He is the only one who knows the direction they need to travel and the things they will and must endure to receive the victory.

You may know **OF** God, but you are demonstrating that you don't **KNOW** Him. Are you truly willing to be a partaker in your children's downfall or eternal damnation? Stop compromising with the devil. Stop sending your children down that wide road of destruction.

REMEMBER: We plant the seed (sow the Word of God). We water the seed (with prayer and faith). But God and only God can bring forth the increase — not you.

As husbands, fathers, daddies, and men, we must pray at all times. If you don't have a relationship with God, however, how can you know what to pray for? Seek His guidance. Begin now.

Spiritual Weapon: Fasting

Some people think that when you fast, you can't eat or drink anything. That is known as a Spiritual Fast and should not be attempted for an extended period of time — unless you have received specific instruction from God to do so. When

Jesus was in the wilderness and fasted, He did not eat; however, scripture does not say He didn't drink anything.

Fruit or Vegetable Fast

You can participate in both at one time or separately. This fast excludes meats, sweets, junk food, or anything fried.

Liquid Fast

This fast consists of consuming water, juice, tea, smoothies, or milkshakes. No sodas or alcoholic beverages are permitted. You can have potato soup, the brew of any other soup, or a combination thereof by mixing or changing them during the fast. If you are going to do this particular fast for a long period, you should make sure you are taking or eating something with protein such as red beans or a baked potato. **NO MEAT** is allowed. If you must have meat, it's best to have poultry such as baked fish, grilled or baked chicken, or turkey.

Meal Removal

A fast can also include not eating breakfast, lunch, OR dinner. At the same time, you must pray about what you are fasting for and read your bible. Stand on those scriptures that apply to whatever you are fasting for.

REMEMBER: Jesus said that some things come through fasting and praying.

If you start a fast and, for some reason, cannot or are unable to complete it, don't condemn yourself; just stop. Always seek God's divine guidance.

Men, as far as your position as the husband is concerned, you should fast on a regular basis. Again, however, I stress that you seek God's and your pastor's guidance and proper instruction on how long the fast should last (the Lord will always confirm His word).

NOTE: Some of you should practice wisdom as well and consult your doctor before beginning a fast of any type.

One More Fast

I refer to the following as a "Sacrifice of Praise" fast.

You can also fast by giving up something you like to do or regularly watch on television such as your favorite soap opera or sitcom. During the fast, you must be in prayer for what you are fasting for (this is when the breakthrough will take place). Whether you are praying for you, your family, the nation, or whatever is in your heart, praying in the Spirit is imperative when you're fasting.

> **REMEMBER:** Praying in the Spirit and your native tongue every day is vitally important.

Pointing Fingers

I'm getting ready to do some toe-stepping here, but please remember everything I state throughout this book is penned with love and concern for the man, woman, and child of God.

STOP blaming the school system for everything your child does at school. As a parent, if you don't exercise your rights about what is being taught or voice your concerns about what is going on in your child's school, then you are leaving it up to the system to teach them any immoral thing they choose. Stand up and be counted for your children. It is the **PARENT'S** responsibility to maintain and teach discipline in the home, not the school system.

Over the last 20 years (a generation), I have observed that a lot of parents are afraid of their children. Our government has given them a free ticket to Hell by letting them say and do whatever they want. If the parent wishes to spank or apply a non-abusive form of discipline, they label it "child abuse" (read Proverbs 23:12-14). The word "beat" has many definitions. One is "to mold into shape," which we can do by using the Word of God — not the abusive form that the world is using. With our government operating under that ignorant spirit of stupidity, we see that their hearts have been hardened. As such, they do not know the difference between constructive correction and physical abuse.

Why is this?

The answer is simple: God has been left out of the equation.

It's best for you to apply the proper form of discipline (which may include spanking) at home. If you don't know how to do that, seek God for instruction.

I Once Was Blind, But Now I See

Let's have a look at a worst-case-scenario when discipline is left in the hands of "the world."

If your child or other loved one is sent to prison, the guards and inmates may find pleasure in abusing them — in essence, gambling with their safety and life. Those with ill-will may find it fun seeing your loved one beaten, molested, raped, dismembered, or killed. I implore you today: Don't let them be able to find joy in abusing your loved one in a "correctional facility."

Let's face it, people: Without God, there is no success. When we leave God out, we operate in the works of failure accompanied by lack of discipline and lack of self-control.

Question: Who was the responsible party that permitted discipline, prayer, and the removal of bibles from our schools?

Answer: Parents, the school board, state representatives, mayors, governors, government officials, and even the church — anyone who didn't stand up for our children.

REMEMBER: The United States of America was founded on prayer, God, and the Holy Bible.

Many, many moons ago, prayer was said at the beginning of school, before school functions and commencement services, and before all sports activities. Now that prayer has been eliminated, those who oppose God are slowly trying to shove God entirely out of our lives and this wonderful country. Man has replaced the Word of God with the way of the devil, which is sin.

Did you know that public schools are permitted to distribute condoms to students without parental consent? That's their way of parenting our children while encouraging "safe sex." The safest sex is no sex at all! Parents, start standing up for your children in their schools. Instill good morals in their lives beginning in the cradle. Please take a stand for their future. Don't continue giving the government total control over their lives by controlling yours.

If we, as a society, continue allowing these things to happen, we are not fighting for our children's moral rights, souls, and salvation. People of God: We must begin by praying for the safety of all children and students. Pray for God to place anointed men and women in the lives of our youth to give them wise counsel and positive direction for their lives.

Don't expect the Parent/Teacher Association to help because they are part of the school system. Their authority only goes so far.

Furthermore, just because a child is out of your home and attending college or is in the military, it does not mean they are mature enough to make wise decisions. They may be out of your home, but they're not out of your life. Be encouraged today in knowing that God watches over you, no matter where you are. He gives you wise counsel that will guide you through life's challenges…and those of your children.

Soul Ties

One thing you must remember is this: When you sleep with someone who's not your spouse, you are taking in the spirits that are operating in that person's life—as well as **ALL** of the spirits that were attached to all of their previous sex partners, dating back to their ancestors. These spirits can be described as either unfamiliar spirits or a generational curse.

These spirits (or demons) typically attach to tangible objects, but when you have sex with a man or woman, your body fluids and spirits have intermingled, connecting you both spiritually and physically. So, the cycle begins. That person likely still has another person's spirits attached to him or her, and those spirits attach to you.

If you are engaged in this type of lifestyle, ask God to forgive you and start over (make sure that both of you ask God for forgiveness for sleeping around before marriage, even if it was with each other). That is another reason why God says not to have sex before marriage. Soul ties can be very destructive to your spirit-man or spirit-woman.

REMEMBER: No matter how much you may love one another, God's Word never changes.

Gentlemen, the first time you sleep with a woman who is not your wife, you are preparing her to become a whore—and you become a whoremonger. When you give her gifts, money, jewelry, etc., then you have introduced her to prostitution and degraded her. How? Just listen to the types of conversations you have with each other or your friends that may sound something like this:

- Her: *"Buy this for me, and I'll give you some."*

- You: *"Man, she's mad at me. Let me get her some flowers and take her out so I can get me some."*
- Her: *"You're not getting any of this…unless you have some money."*
- Her: *"You have to prove you love me first."*
- Her: *"She may have the man, but I have his money."*
- Her: *"I have three children to take care of."*
- Friend: *"It's almost Christmas. Get with her and buy her children some toys…and then get you some."*

REMEMBER: When either of you chooses to go your separate ways, both of you will begin searching for another victim to fill that void. You will then enter into an endless cycle of unsatisfied "sexcapades," and she has been left with a bad name, for lust has entered in, and she's been stripped of her self-respect.

If your significant other stops giving you some or stops doing things for you just so they can get you to buy something or take them somewhere, that is a form of manipulation. Recognize it for what it is! A spirit of witchcraft has now been activated by using the spirits of deception and manipulation.

Too many men have brought this lifestyle into their marriage by making their whore or prostitute their wife. It's time to restore the respect and dignity to that special woman in your life. Stop putting the woman in control and help her become the help-meet (wife) she is supposed to be.

The Spirit of the Lord explained "help-meet" to me this way: *"The phrase help-meet does not go together like so many people SAY. "Help" means she was created to help man in fulfilling his purpose, as well as helping him to keep things running smoothly and to assist wherever needed. "Meet" simply states that everything the man needs can be found in her as a spiritual helper and physical companion; having someone to love, as well as sharing his life and prosperity with"* (see Genesis 2:20-23).

More Details About Soul Ties

Do you find yourself still thinking about your ex from time to time? If so, maybe you're still connected to them through a soul tie.

How?

Perhaps you are still in possession of clothing, jewelry, gifts, or something else given to you by them. Those "things" are still connected to you by soul ties. Even if you stop having sex with that person or if they die, you still carry those spirits with you. They may also be transferred to your children and future generations.

REMEMBER: Spirits never die; they just find another body to inhabit or something else to attach itself to.

Soul ties can affect you emotionally, to the point where you still have a desire to be with that person. Do you find yourself having a hard time breaking that attachment? It's likely there's a spirit within you that's fearful of letting go. As it relates to a lover or sex partner, your spirit became one with them. You have given each other's spirits things that make you still connected as one.

If you are still in possession of material things that connect you with your past sex partner and can't or don't want to get rid of it, give it to God. Place those things at His feet and let Him deliver you from the attachment. You may have to take it to your pastor to have it blessed or anointed — especially antiques or things passed down from family to family through the years.

SIDEBAR: Don't let the ignorance of man or the foolishness of scientists lead you to believe you evolved from an animal. You do **NOT** derive from apes. Man has divided everything on earth as either an animal, vegetable, or mineral. **YOU** are a spirit that lives in a body. You have a soul. You were created in the image of God and designed by Him to live and praise Him all the days of your life (see Genesis 1:27; 2:26; 1 John 4:4).

The Father and the Daddy: The Difference

Have you ever wondered where the custom of the father giving away the bride came from? The answer is: From God Almighty! He made a woman (Eve, His daughter) and presented her to Adam. It is the same as a father giving away his daughter to his future son-in-law (your son-**UNDER**-the-law). Our Lord and Savior Jesus Christ is a positive image of God (His Father), as well as a role model of who we are to become.

What is a "Father"?

The father is the one who plants the seed in the woman and impregnates her. The woman is an incubator. Although the father's seed fertilized the egg, whatever affects her body or whatever goes on around her can affect the personality and physical/mental outcome of the child as well.

In many cases, the biological father is not always around. Some of them run for the hills or say, *"That's not my baby!"* All the while and leading up to momentous occasions (such as graduation), he failed to support that child in any way—financially, contact via in person or phone, nor taking an interest in extra-curricular activities in the child's life.

But these same men are also quick to stick out their chests when their children graduate or gain success. It is then that the deadbeat will proudly profess, *"That's **MY** child!"*

Men, learn the true meaning of being a man of God. Teach your sons the importance of a relationship with God before he starts dating. Let them know it's okay to remain a virgin until he's married, whether his friends agree or not (if they don't respect that decision, they were never really friends in the first place). Stop telling your sons the four "Fs" that you learned from the streets:

1. Find them
2. Fool them.
3. Forget them.
4. And the other "F-word" I will not mention here.

Men of bad character give all men a bad name. Proverbs 15:7 says, *"The lips of the wise disperse knowledge; but the heart of the foolish doeth not so."* Are **YOU** a fool?

Teach your daughters how important it is to have respect for God by respecting herself and her body. Invest **TIME** in your children's lives by studying and sharing the Word of God with them daily.

If you haven't spent time with your children recently, make time. Even if you have children from another relationship, make time for them as well. Make yourself available for those moments when your children will need your support. As the head, they will look to you to grow, be loved, and feel secure. At the same time, don't neglect your wife and children at home. They are your first responsibility. If you are having difficulty navigating the "two lives," take the matter before God and let Him work it out. The Word of God says, *"He who provides against his own home is worse than an infidel [one who does not believe in a religious faith such as Christianity]"* (1 Timothy 5:8).

If you are in a situation where you and the children's mother do not get along (for whatever the reason, to include divorce), please don't disown your children. Stand up and be a real father—a positive role model they can look up to...an image of what a man of God really is. Don't scar them by being the absent father, as you may never get the opportunity to parent again properly. Remember that God is watching you and is holding you accountable.

If you have been restricted from seeing your children by the law, get your act right and seek the Lord in prayer with a sincere heart. God may open the doors for you to see them—in His time; not yours. Meanwhile, continue to pray for them and their mother. Your children are not a liability but rather an asset to you, their mother, the children's future, and especially to God!

Don't come bearing gifts to buy your child's love. Find out what they need and supply that need. For example, if it's something for school, help by purchasing clothes, books, and other essentials. Whatever you've done for them in the past, never throw it back in their face by saying things like:

- *"After all I've done for you, and this is how you repay me?"*
- *"I worked two jobs to send you to school."*
- *"I did whatever I had to do."*
- *"You selfish, little…"*
- *"You're so ungrateful!"*

That is not wise parenting or mature. That is the voice of a selfish, ungrateful spirit operating in your life. Whatever you've done should have been out of both love and responsibility.

I'm going to note here two tragic events that can happen to a child in his or her life:

1. When a child doesn't know who their birth father is or any good thing about him. This often happens because the woman deceived the father into thinking the child was his when, if fact, the child is another man's, OR the woman is pregnant, never divulges that fact to the father, and walks away from the relationship.
2. When the child knows who the father is, but the man doesn't want anything to do with him or her.

Why are these tragedies? Because the child has been abandoned and confusion sets in. Have you ever considered the vast number of children who have no idea who their birth father or mother is? The harsh reality is that they may be sleeping with their blood brother or sister! The greatest fear is that they may marry and have children of their own.

What is a "Daddy"?

Whatever counsel the father gives children is the act of a daddy. Always be mindful that God is holding you responsible for the proper upbringing of that child, no matter how old they are.

If they live with you, then your responsibility is to train them in every area of life. If they do not reside with you, you are still obligated to share God's Word with them. Lead by example. Children are very cognizant of more than we often give them credit for from a young age.

Whatever spirits are operating in the parents' lives can be transferred to the children. Matthew 12:35 reminds us, *"A good man out of the good treasures of the heart brings forth good things; an evil man out of the evil treasures of his heart brings forth evil things."* The Word of God also says that a tree is known by its fruit.

Every day, there are countless men—young and old—that enter into a woman's life. How many of them have been equipped and trained to become a husband, father, dad, and man of God?

REMEMBER: The dad helps in training the children in the way they should go. He counsels, instructs, and keeps the house in order. He is the authority figure in the home. He knows how to apply love and discipline.

Dads, God is holding you responsible for what you teach your sons and daughters. It doesn't matter if your father, mother, or guardian raised you in the ways of the Lord or not. God has provided you with the gateway to manhood. Stop refusing to follow Him. He has given you a blueprint of a lifestyle to live by: The Holy Bible. The bible is your roadmap to becoming the father, dad, husband, and man of God He and your family need you to be.

If you are compromising, then you don't know God; you just know of Him. If you **DO** know Him, stop straddling the fence. We have placed ourselves in this catastrophe because of pride and listening to other men who don't know the true meaning of what it is to be a real man. Then, there are some of you who have been under the leadership of a woman for so long, you don't know how to lead. You have fallen into Satan's trap by giving him control of the relationship through the woman.

I can't help but think about people whose desire and focus are on professional athletes, movie stars, models, etc. Why long for that type of relationship if that "star" is unwilling to give their life to the **LORD**? With the instantaneous nature of media as it is today, as soon as that "star" does something wrong, all fingers point at them, their name is tarnished and degraded, and their lives fall into a state of confusion. What's amazing about our God is that God is willing to meet them where they are (even in a downtrodden state) to draw them to Him!

There are far too many celebrities who are wrapped up in the things of this world such as their homes, cars, money, sex, and fame. Many will say, *"I made it! I worked hard to get here!"* But wait: You can't do anything without God, for it was **HIM** who gave the power to get wealth (read Deuteronomy 8:18-20).

Take a moment to look deeply at the faces of celebrities, and you will see how unhappy many of them really are. Some have lost sight of God's purpose for them in order to live the lifestyle they now have. The money and fame have become their god, but it is **GOD** who said **HE** would supply our every need! They must either turn back to God or get to know Him for themselves. When they do, they will find that they cannot be happy without Him. There is a void in everyone's heart that can only be filled with God's Spirit, and nothing else will do!

If you are a celebrity and reading this book, do yourself a favor and **KEEP YOUR CLOTHES ON!** Stop being a fool for the devil. Your salvation is not judged by how much money you make, how much money you give to your favorite charity, how much you give to the poor, your good deeds, what you do in the community, or even the amount of your tithes and offering. None of those things will save your soul. **JESUS** is the only way to God. **HE** is the only mediator between God and man.

REMEMBER: Your salvation is not based on things of this world (read Matthew 6:19-21).

This is a daily walk. Each day, you will be challenged or put to the test by confronting sin, and it will come in many ways. You don't have to go looking for it because it waits for you around every corner. We are encouraged in scripture this way:

"Be strong and of good courage; trust in the Lord, and He will see you through" (Joshua 1:7-8). Verse nine goes a little deeper: *"Have I not commanded thee? Be strong and of good courage..."*

A Note About Discipline

Some parents become very defensive when it comes to disciplining children by the biological parent or the parent of a recent marriage. It must be noted here that there is no such thing as a "step" mother, father, son, daughter, sister, or brother. Once you marry someone with children who are not yours, you become a *family*.

A Mother's Role

I'm going to get right to the meat of the matter here: If you are pregnant, please don't abort your child. Don't send him or her back home to God early. Give them time to fulfill their purpose here on earth.

REMEMBER: Abortion is a selfish act of murder.

Think about this: Did we ask to be born? Even now, movies are being made relating to this topic. Some people have had near-death experiences, visions, or dreams about that question.

Your children are gifts from God. Some of you may not have wanted children, but **GOD** permitted them to be conceived and birthed. To that end, never tell your children they were a "mistake." You didn't make a "mistake" when you had sex. Both of you knew the possibility of you getting pregnant. Stop telling yourself and others that lie when the truth is that both of you gave in to your lustful desires and your sin was exposed. For God to permit you to get pregnant means that He has a purpose for that child. You were **GOD'S** choice to birth that child through that man.

REMEMBER: Give your children those parts of you that they need the most: your love, time, wisdom, and most of all, a means of identity, direction, and guidance through the Word of God.

Time with God is NOT Optional

When it comes time to go to church, some of you men will say things like:

- *"I have to wash my car today."*
- *"I'm going fishing with the guys."*
- *"The game comes on at 12:00, and church doesn't let out until 1:00."*
- *"All the pastor wants is my money."*

What you're really saying is that God and your family are not important to you. Putting other things before your relationship with God has caused the spirit of idolatry to abide within you. You have made those other things your god (read Matthew 12:36-37; 6:19-23). Professional sports are often played

I Once Was Blind, But Now I See

on Sundays. Record the game and go into the house of the Lord to praise and worship Him! During the off-season, you have **NO** excuse.

If you don't have to work on Sunday (or whatever day you worship), go to church with your family. If you do have to work on that day, pray and ask God to change your schedule so that you can fellowship at your house of worship.

Listen, there's nothing wrong with watching church service on television, listening on the radio or internet, or communicating through emails, texts, and social media. However, it should not take the place of frequenting the church house that God wants you to be in.

If you are a man full of excuses, there will come a time when you will wonder why nothing is working out for you. The main reason is that you have become deaf to the voice of God. Another reason might be that you're not seeking Him for direction. Another reason could be that you're not supporting the church financially.

REMEMBER: God cannot open the windows of Heaven if you haven't sent anything up so that He can send something down! If you're not giving to God, then you are operating in lack. Your lack of sowing can even cause you bad health…
or worse.

What does this mean?

If you want God to take care of your house and supply your needs, take care of **HIS** needs first.

Think about the following scenarios and their outcomes as it relates to sowing financial seeds into God's kingdom. See if you can relate.

- ➤ You paid your car note with a financial seed meant for God. As a result, your car continues to break down, or it becomes harder to make the payments in the coming months.
- ➤ You bought groceries with a financial seed meant for God. As a result, the food may spoil fast, and you have to throw it away, or you don't have enough money left for "fill-in" groceries during the month.
- ➤ You purchased new clothes with a financial seed meant for God. As a result, something happens that totally ruins them or someone comes along and steals them.

Anything and everything you spend money on in place of sowing seeds into God's Kingdom places you in the wilderness a little while longer. Don't leave an open door for Satan to come in and steal your money because he will cause you to spend it foolishly.

REMEMBER: Sow willingly…or it may not count. God loves a cheerful giver. You can hide your true feelings from man, but you can **NEVER** hide them from God!

Follow the life of Jesus. He was a humble man and obedient to God in every way. If you believe that you can't be or live like Him, then you're correct! No man can live like Jesus because Jesus must first live inside of you. Then and only then can you live the life that Christ lived, as He lives in and through you. There is no man or woman that God has used to do His will and prepared the way for our Lord and Savior Jesus Christ who was perfect. They all had issues! Therefore, there's no reason for you to live with excuses such as:

- *"I'm not Jesus."*
- *"It's because I'm black."*
- *"It's the white man's fault."*
- *"I come from the projects."*
- *"I have all these children."*
- *"I'm too old."*
- *"I'm a pimp."*
- *"I'm a prostitute."*
- *"I was raped by my daddy."*
- *"I slept with my mother."*

All throughout the Holy Bible, God used those who have gone through things to show others where they came from. The Word is used to show **YOU** where He can take you. That's why we **ALL** have a testimony!

The Outcome of Sin

Let's take a look at some of the men and women in the Holy Bible who were used by God in a mighty way to fulfill His purpose.

- ➢ **Noah:** In the Book of Genesis, God made a covenant with Noah because Noah found grace in the eyes of God (Genesis 6:8). He promised Noah that he would not destroy the earth by water again. As proof, God placed his bow in the sky (we call it a rainbow) (see Genesis 8:21-22). However, after the earth had dried, Noah and his family exited the ark, he planted a vineyard, made himself some wine from the fruit of the vine, and became drunk. Still, God showed Noah mercy and blessed him with favor and long life (Noah died at the age of 950 years old). Read Genesis 6:8; 9:8-9, 29.

- **Abram/Abraham:** After the death of Abram's father, God told Abram to get out of his father's house, leave the country, and get far away from his relatives. When he left, he brought along his nephew, Lot, all of Lot's possessions, and Lot's family. God did **NOT** tell Abram to do that (see Genesis 12:1-3). Lot also lied when he said his wife was his sister, for she was his half-sister *AND* wife (if he had told that she was his wife, he was afraid he would be killed, and that she would be taken away from him). After some time passed, Abram gave in to his wife's (Sarai's) suggestion and took her maid as a wife. From this union, Ishmael was born, but he was not the child God promised to Abram. It came to pass that God kept His promise and gave Abram a son through his wife (who is now called Sarah). Isaac was the son God promised to Abraham.
- **Moses:** This man was a murderer. He killed an Egyptian, hid the body, and ran away. After 40 years had passed, God told Moses to return to Egypt. At the time, Moses had low self-esteem and a speech impediment. He tried to find any excuse he could not to have God send him back to Egypt (see Exodus 6:30). God used him to bring forth a great feast before Pharaoh (see Exodus 7:10). Continue reading the next couple chapters of Exodus to learn about the plagues on Egypt. Moses was also used by God to bring the Hebrews out of Egypt and into the

Promised Land. Moses was also chosen by God to receive the Ten Commandments (see Exodus 20:1-19). After all of the great miracles that Moses performed, he was not permitted to enter into the Promised Land due to his disobedience; he struck a rock twice instead of speaking to it—as God instructed.

- **The Disciples:** *"After His disciples had been with Him for a long time, they finally confessed that they believed He was sent from God"* (John 16:30). In verse 32, Jesus tells them that they will all go their way and abandon Him. *"The night that Judas betrayed Jesus with a kiss, the soldiers asked for Jesus, and He [Jesus] said, "I am He." When Jesus spoke these words, the soldiers fell backward to the ground"* (John 18:6). Judas had a background not many people discuss. He had stolen 30 pieces of silver from the treasury, so his grand idea was to turn Jesus in to replace what he stole. See? Even **JESUS** had people around Him who meant him no good! God will even use someone who's evil to get **HIS** will done, for without Judas' thievery and deceitful ways, Jesus would not have been betrayed.

REMEMBER: As long as you live, there is time for repentance, salvation, and forgiveness.

NOTE: There is no such thing as "Purgatory" after you die; there's only Heaven or Hell. Purgatory is a place or state of suffering for the purification of the souls of the dead who will eventually be worthy of Heaven and is a Roman Catholic belief. This religious myth will lead you down that wide path to Hell. The only place you can relate to Purgatory is earth because this is the only place you live before you die where you can pray for yourself, your family, your relatives, and your friends' salvation through our **LORD** and our **SAVIOR** Jesus the Christ.

If you could pray your way into Heaven (God's Kingdom), then God would have told you how many prayers it would take to get there (see Proverbs 3:5,7).

If your good deeds were the way into Heaven, then God would let you know the point value and what system He uses (see Isaiah 64:6). Scripture tells us that our good deeds are as filthy rags.

If getting in touch with your inner-self was the way into Heaven, we wouldn't need Jesus (see Proverbs 16:18). Pride, after all, is a self-righteous spirit. Our inner-self is corrupt because of our sinful nature, and our spirit is unclean.

REMEMBER: God still loves you. Go to Him in prayer. He's waiting to receive you unto Himself.

- **Samson:** One of Samson's problems was the lust of the eyes. He was raised as a Nazarite, which meant he was not supposed to take of the fruit of the vine, touch anything that was dead, or get his hair cut (see Numbers 6:1-9). Samson killed his enemies with the jawbone of an ass. He also drank wine, became drunk, and told where his strength came from: his hair. His enemies then cut off his hair! In his lust for the beautiful and seductive Delilah, Samson's disobedience cost him his anointing, his hair, his sight, and eventually his life. However, God loved him and restored his hair and anointing. God still used Samson's great strength to bring down the pillars of the arena in which he killed 3,000 Philistines at one time (read Judges 16:23-30).

- ➢ **David:** He was the man who used his slingshot and stone to kill Goliath and then cut off the giant's head with the giant's own sword. He was also a musician (he played the harp) and slew a lion and a bear (read 1 Samuel 17:36-37;49-51). However, he was another man who let the enticement of a beautiful woman entangle him in a web of lust. Overtaken by his desire, he committed adultery. Because of this seductive spirit, she became pregnant. To cover up the infidelity, David had the woman's husband sent into battle, knowing that he would be killed, so that he could have her for himself. Still, God used David to write the Books of Psalms, 1 Samuel, and 2 Samuel as well. After much soul-searching and repenting, David became the apple of God's eye.

God is very well aware of your past. He was with you and kept you through it all. Go to Him and ask for forgiveness. Repent (turn away from, having no desire to do "it" anymore), and He will forgive you.

Accept Jesus as your Lord and personal Savior. Share your testimony with others so that they may hear of the awesomeness of God and your salvation. Pray that through your testimonies, your family, friends, and others may be saved from Hell and the eternal Lake of Fire, for we overcome Satan by the blood of the Lamb (Jesus) and the words of our testimony!

Distractions and Victory

Most women are aware of the spirit of persuasion that they possess. The woman was made from man's side, for she was a part of him. When the woman (Eve, Adam's wife) listened to a third party (the serpent) that gave her unwise counsel in her marriage, it introduced the beginnings of a spirit of division in man. After being deceived by the conversation with the serpent, Eve became enticed by the beauty of the fruit (read Genesis 3:6; Proverbs 3:5-7). By Adam being a partaker in the conversation between Eve and the serpent, Adam surrendered his will of following God's commandment by submitting to his wife's request (he also found the fruit pleasing to the eyes) (see Genesis 2:16-17).

Some men and women use the spirit of persuasion to deceive, trick or enhance the beauty of something. In response, we can become so intrigued by what's being said, we think it's okay to take part in what's being done. This, too, falls under the spirit of witchcraft.

Speaking from a man's point of view, the desire for a woman is inviting. The woman was not only made **FOR** man but **FROM** man as well. Her beauty and her body were made for man to look upon as an attraction and to desire appropriately: to fulfill the desires of your heart as a **WIFE**, as well as fulfilling the spoken Word of God, meaning she is to reproduce after our own kind.

However, Satan has corrupted God's plan with a spirit of seduction, lust, and control. These spirits are a distraction and have caused many men to stray away from the true nature and purpose of having a woman.

Many women wear very revealing clothing and skimpy swimsuits. Some do those things to flaunt what they have. Others go to bars, lounges, nightclubs, and casinos on the hunt for a man, his money, or to get laid. Then, there are still others who degrade themselves and take it to the extreme by posing and modeling naked for magazines and billboards. They make pornographic moves and become prostitutes for themselves, pimps, or escort services. Some call it a "job"; others call it a "career" (see Proverbs 3:5-8).

Gentlemen, be honest: Do you **REALLY** have respect for a woman who degrades herself while she's in that tumultuous time of her life? If you are honest, the truth is that you only desire her for what she can do for or give to you. There is no respect involved; just lust to help you "get one off." When you tell her how fine she looks and you say it with lust in your heart, it's like getting her father's approval. In fact, you are giving her the approval of the 'Father of Lies': Satan. Clearly, she is operating in Satan's will and not the will of God.

If you encounter a woman living that type of lifestyle and you desire to have her as your girlfriend or wife, make sure **GOD** has placed that desire in your heart. God is not going to give you a play-by-play script of what's needed or what He needs to do to get you from boyfriend/girlfriend to husband/wife. That woman just may be the woman you need to get you on the right track—and you just may be the right man to turn her life around.

Men, never put these women down or condemn them. A lot of them may have been forced into that situation. Some have been so severely abused, they have lost their self-respect and feel empty inside because they never knew or experienced true love from their father, mother, or anyone else in their lives. Maybe they have never been told or trained on how to be a respectable person. They may not know what love is, what God's love is, or even **WHO** God is.

Ladies, if you continue to live or function in that type of lifestyle, realize that God will hold you responsible for the enticement and seduction of the men and woman you cause to fall into lust. If you have publicly exposed yourself in any magazines, television programs, or movies that have enticed men or women into a life of lust and sex, God will hold you accountable.

Men, please don't entertain the lustful spirits that are attached to those women. Avoid their conversations at all costs (read Proverbs 5:1-13). If God leads you into a discussion with them, you will know because you will use His Word, not your money or sexual innuendos.

You are a light shining in the darkness. Don't let the darkness consume you. (Read Psalm 112:4; Mark 8:36).

Be also aware that there are women who are innocent. They simply look good in anything they wear and are not trying to entice anyone. Satan knows this and will not hesitate to use them as well, so always be on your guard.

I Once Was Blind, But Now I See

Men, the same applies to you as well. Don't be a fool for the devil. Don't pose nude in magazines and movies. Don't wear pants so tight that the imprint of your size can be seen.

Why?

Because God will also hold you accountable as well, for there are millions of men and women who you are enticing into lust, sex, and masturbation.

REMEMBER: With every temptation, God has already made a way of escape. Pray in the Name of Jesus and ask God for strength. If you have already given in to temptation, pray in the Name of Jesus and ask Him to forgive you as well as the women you have enticed or seduced.

REMEMBER: Men, you are leaders. Set an example.
Guard your heart with the Word of God.
Be led by wisdom, not lustful desires.

Take a moment right now to examine your heart. Reflect on the examples you are setting for your children. Maybe you've been the one guilty of provoking lust. Search your heart. Ask yourself:

- Would you like your wife, daughter, son, or even mother to dress inappropriately?
- Is enticement worth the risk of potentially being sexually assaulted by someone?
- Do the long-term after-effects feel good after you've participated in lustful pleasures?

I cannot stress enough that these familiar spirits will be passed down to your children from generation to generation. Each time, it will grow progressively worse.

REMEMBER: This is another avenue that Satan uses that can or will cause the children to die young. The generational curse, familiar spirit, and transference of spirit must be stopped. It begins with **YOU**.

Misled

Look at how the movie industry, social media, and video games have permitted the showing of adultery, vulgar language, nudity, same-sex partners, and perverted sex (such as with animals). In addition, some R-rated movies are just as bad as MRA-rated (Mature Rated Audience) and X-rated screenings. In so many ways, they show that it's okay to sleep around, have children cussing out and disrespecting their parents, and other immoral behaviors.

And we are left wondering why children act the way they do? *Hmm...*

Parents, in some cases, your children are overindulging in watching cartoons. Are you fully aware of what they're actually watching? Do you monitor the contents or just assume that it's a cartoon, so it's just fine for your children? In today's times, our youth are now playing games on their phones and chatting online — but with whom? A lot of the content in the cartoons and games of today lack morals. Think about it. The soul you help save could be your own, your children's, and future generations to come! Be aware!

Men, if you're shacking up, you are already in violation and endangering not only your soul but also the souls of everyone else in the home and those who see you living that lifestyle. What you may not realize is that you're given them an open invitation to an early death by displaying that it's okay to defy God's commands and do the will of Satan. Once again, you have unleashed familiar and unfamiliar spirits into their lives, including generational curses, lust, low self-esteem, and so much more.

REMEMBER: Familiar spirits are those that are attached to you and follow you and your family. Unfamiliar spirits are those that you or your family don't recognize. They may come from others whom you or your loved ones have slept with or are in close association with.

NOTE: Everything they've seen you do, and everything they've heard you say has already been transferred into their spirit. Even after your children reach the age of accountability, you are still responsible for their spiritual and moral growth, along with their overall wellbeing.

Many of the children today were conceived in lust, not love. A wide variety of scenarios could have been presented at the moment leading up to the intimate moment that led to conception such as:

- Being angry with your significant other, so you cheated on him or her.
- Partying and felt the desire to have sex.
- Being drunk.
- Being high on drugs.

- Loneliness.
- Getting married just to be able to have "moral" sex.
- Saying "yes" just to keep from hurting the other person's feelings.

Changing lanes here…

Parents, your son or daughter may have a child out of wedlock and leave that child in your care. Once again, the spirits of low self-esteem, lack of commitment, immaturity, abandonment, and unwise counsel are at play. It is **NOT** your job to take care of your child's responsibility. Now, I'm not referring to Spring or Summer breaks and babysitting while the parent works. I'm talking about it not being your job to take charge of, raise, or keep them while your son or daughter goes out and lives it up as if they are not a parent—potentially impregnating or getting pregnant again!

If they need help, by all means: Get them some help! Avoid becoming your grandchildren's legal guardian while your child walks away from his or her responsibilities to that child.

Sometimes, men raised by their mother in a single-parent household can be crippled by her overprotective spirit that was brought on by her emotions and selfishness. Her motherly instinct is to nurture and protect, which can cause the following repercussions:

- She will not allow him to be disciplined or punished.
- She hides them when they're in trouble, whether from the other parent or the law.

- She takes their side against the other parent.
- She gives them money or other means to help them run away.
- She keeps an open-door policy and allows him to come home for mama to take care of him.

There's an old saying that relates to mothers from years ago that states: *"You must cut the apron string and let him be a man."* However, the cutting of the apron string is not the problem.

Why?

1. Women cannot train a man on how to be a man because she's not a man!
2. You must seek God on how to raise him.
3. If no man in his life knows God or can lead him in the right direction, then you must give him totally back to God. In God's time, He will send you and your son the right man of God that both of you need. If not, God will guide you through. All you have to do is ask Him for that guidance.

REMEMBER: What you speak and teach him will have a lasting impact on him. If you are continuing to call him your "baby" when he's older than 10 years old, then the enemy can use that as a form of a crutch later in his life, knowing that he can always call on you for help—and it doesn't matter if it's you or another woman that he calls on to take care of him.

Let's look at another scenario.

Maybe your son doesn't have his own place, but his girlfriend does. He goes to her place to have some of his needs met and then comes to your home to eat you out of house and home. He then wants to tell you how to run your house and may even get angry if you can't meet his needs as expected. He may even have the nerve to ask you to let his girlfriend move in and live with both of you!

Listen up: A "baby" cannot take care of himself. As such, when you keep calling him a baby, you may not mean it in the literal sense, but the enemy will use it to his advantage. Meanwhile, neither mother nor son realizes it was a trap set by Satan long ago, and it began with some of the following sentiments:

- *"But he's just a boy."*
- *"He's too young to understand."*
- *"He's not very bright when it comes to these things."*
- *"But he's my baby."*
- *"He can stay with me as long as he needs to."*
- *"Why do you want to get married? Stay here with mama."*
- *"She's just trying to trap you."*
- *"Mama will send you some money every week."*
- *"Don't worry: This will be our little secret. Daddy doesn't have to know."*
- *"Don't worry: Mama will take care of it."*
- *"I'll get the money somehow."*
- *"Mama knows what's best for her baby."*
- *"He's my son. No man can tell me how to raise him."*
- *"No man will come before my child."*

I Once Was Blind, But Now I See

REMEMBER: Sometimes, a man will get attached to a woman who has her own, then they move in together. What he has to realize is that it's her place, not his.

What happens when she evicts him? Where will he go? With whom will he stay? I suppose "baby" can go back home to mama...

Many men (especially black men) have a business mind, but they use it for the wrong things or in the wrong way. It doesn't help to have someone — often a wife or girlfriend — who discourages them by hinting at the man not being smart enough.

How about some advice?

Before you approach your wife or girlfriend with your idea, take it to the Lord in prayer and ask that it goes well with her. In most cases, the answer to your prayer will come in the form of the support you seek, and you will be encouraged to press on.

Men, remember you were not called to be a stay-at-home dad. You were called to work, be a leader, and a role model of Jesus.

Consider Adam in the Garden of Eden. He had a job to do. He wasn't just lying around doing nothing all day every day. He was working and tending to the garden.

Jesus the Christ was a leader and perfect example of God. He lived His life doing well to everyone and spreading the love of God to all mankind.

Men, this is spiritual warfare. You must prepare yourself for battle. To learn what you have to do, read Ephesians 6:10-18. I'll share the first two verses here:

"Finally, my brother, be strong in the Lord, and in the power of His might. Put on the whole armor of God that ye may be able to stand against the wiles of the devil."

Now, you take it from here and read the rest of the passage!

Praying in the Spirit

Every child of God should pray in the Spirit. It is your prayer language against the enemy. It also helps in making the right decisions. How can you expect the Christ in you to operate at His fullest if you deny the Gifts of the Spirit? When you pray in the Spirit, **ONLY GOD** can understand what you are saying because your spirit-man/spirit-woman is in tune with the Holy Spirit (see Romans 8:26-27) — unless you are in the presence of someone with the Gift of Interpretation of Tongues (see 1 Corinthians 12:10).

When you were born, you spoke in tongues — baby-talk, which is a language of innocence and purity. The same applies when you pray in the Spirit.

Let's follow the example set by Jesus. He would seek God in **ALL** things. He prayed constantly and used wisdom in making decisions. In that same manner, so should we. Jesus was all man—*AND* all God. Every desire of man was within Him, but He disciplined Himself in the will of His Father. Jesus experienced every temptation we have (and others we have not, but someone else has).

You can no longer "blame it on the white man" (as many of you who are reading this do). The blame should be placed on your own foolish pride and selfish ways because those attributes are what is holding you back and keeping you suffering from an unforgiving heart towards those who have done spiritual, mental, emotional, and physical harm to your ancestors. This lack of understanding in God is a stupid spirit of pride and prejudice. If you're not blaming your own kind, then you're placing the blame on other immigrants by saying they're taking all of the jobs. If you must, learn another language so that you can compete in the job market!

REMEMBER: Your unforgiving heart will keep you in bondage and poverty and from accomplishing your goals in life. Your unforgiveness will keep you out of Heaven, too.

It must be noted here that I am not putting the African American community down. These are all things I've experienced and still see ongoing in society.

I am not blinded to the fact that racism is alive and well. Trust me when I say: God will take care of the haters. We can't defeat them all by fighting them on our own. Racists can be found from the interior of the White House on down. They operate in the flesh, and we cannot defeat them in the flesh. We must gear up and defeat them in the spirit realm. We must tear their kingdom down by applying the Word of God. A lot of things that are done by racists are meant to pacify us. Well, as we "accept" their pacifiers, let us continue to wage spiritual warfare on them—and watch **GOD** move!

If this makes you angry, **GOOD!** Get angry enough to make and be the **CHANGE!** Your change begins when you learn how to fight. You can't learn how to fight until you are taught. You can't be taught unless you study the Word of God. You can't study the Word of God unless you can understand it. You can't understand it unless you rightly divide it. You can't rightly divide it unless you let the Holy Spirit teach you.

Pray in Jesus' Name. Let him show you what church to attend or who to talk to so that you can learn to fight with the Word. Go to God in prayer and ask Him to show what He has placed in you to make a difference in your life, your family's life, and the lives of others in this world. It's important to keep in mind that whatever you do with the gifts and dreams God has given you, He will hold you responsible for them—whether you use them or not.

When you decide to make a change, you will lose a lot of so-called friends and even relatives as well. Still, set an example. Rise! In seeking God in **ALL** things, ask Him how to dress on any given day, what to eat, what to watch on television, which movies to see at the theater, what type of music you should listen to, and what clothes to buy. Stop compromising with the devil.

I Once Was Blind, But Now I See

Oh! And don't be surprised when God answers you concerning those things.

You may be able to change others' way of thinking by pointing them in the right direction...if you allow God to guide your thoughts with His wisdom. For example:

- If you sell drugs, you have the potential to be a real businessman.
- If you mix drugs, you have the potential to be a pharmacist.
- If you mix drinks, you have the potential to be a chemist and develop a new cure for diseases.
- If you argue a lot, you have the potential to be a lawyer.
- If you know how to get women to sell their bodies, you have the potential to be a counselor.

Don't laugh. Those things are not impossible or too far-fetched! After all, you don't know what purpose God has for you until you ask Him.

Men, just as a woman should strive to be a virgin until she marries, so should you. Yes: **YOU**, too! Actually, when you stop having sex until you're married, you spiritually become a virgin all over again. As such, if you're engaged, stop having sex until your honeymoon. Allow God to clean up your body and spirit as you prepare to wed. If you truly love each other, then wait. Submit yourselves unto the Lord. Resist the devil, and he will flee!

A message to the ladies: The phrase *"No ring; no thing"* does not mean your mate will marry you. A ring (engagement) is not a license to have sexual relations. Instead, tell him, *"After the 'I do,' then we will do!"* In the interim, give your bodies and desires to God, and He will keep you. If you don't have self-control now, what do you think will happen after you get married?

Men, drop that tired, old line that goes, *"If you love me, you will give me some."* **STOP IT!** The same goes for you: Self-control is very important to you now and in the marriage. If you are continually having pre-marital sex (which is fornication), it can destroy your body. It can even make you old before your time by making you appear 60 years old…when you're only forty! Fornication can cause sicknesses such as cancer and AIDS. 1 Corinthians 6:18-19 says that you have sinned against your body!

Don't bring old baggage into your new relationship or marriage. If you are a man or woman who is abusive towards your partner, be loving enough to walk away from the relationship and get your healing before attempting to get involved with someone else. If you are a victim of abuse, let your partner go until he or she gets healed from whatever abuse exposure they had in their past. If they were in love with God first, then they would know what love is and not abuse you.

Learn from your mistakes and bad decisions. Seek God and ask what you must do as you gain both wisdom and understanding.

Let God prepare both of you for your new future together. Give Him the chance to give you the victory!

Some reasons why children are being misled and dying so young are because of:

- Disobedience to God, parents, teachers, and others in positions of authority.
- Drug abuse.
- Hot tempers.
- Jealousy.
- Domestic violence at the hands of their boyfriend/girlfriend.
- Sex at a young age.

They all fall under the spirits of abuse, pride, and jealousy. Remember, too, that cussing is also a contributing factor. It can bring about sickness and disease—the leading cause of early deaths in our youth. Do you want their lives to be shortened by minutes, hours, days, weeks, or years because they cannot control their tongue? Teach them what the Word of God says about there being death and life in the power of the tongue.

Minister Aaron Weaver

A Prayer for Leadership

My Father, my Lord, my God:

Teach me and train me on how to become the man you have called me to be, the husband I must become, and the daddy who uses wisdom to govern the family.

Father, as you train and develop me into the leader, prophet, priest, and king you have ordained me to be, guide me with Your Spirit and give me the wisdom to make the right decisions. Most of all, God, let me lead by example.

Father, help me to give wise counsel to my family and to teach others the same. Grant me the wisdom to educate those in intimate relationships to respect themselves and to show them the right way to grow and live according to Your Word.

In Jesus' Name,

Amen.

Chapter 3

Disciplined

In the Book of Hebrews 12:7-8, it speaks of the love of God in this way: If God didn't love you, He wouldn't discipline you, for He chastens those whom He loves.

Discipline and self-control should first be implemented in the home, instilled in us by our parents or guardian, as growth and maturity take place. Discipline is the very first stage of obedience. The voice of discipline must be followed to be successful. My wife said it like this: *"Much God, much success; no God, no success."* They may seem like only words to you, but within is much wisdom.

We must realize that relationships are built as respect is earned. Respect is both critical and essential for a prosperous and productive marriage, as well as strong relationships with family—especially when serving God.

When we apply discipline, there's no reason for a power struggle to determine who's in charge or (as some people say) who wears the pants in the family. If you're looking for a prosperous marriage and relationship, let **GOD** wear the pants…let **HIM** be in control!

Your home must have a divine structure:

- ➤ The husband as the leader, head, and authority figure.
- ➤ The wife as the one with divine influence and the encourager for you and the children.

Counseling is a must before you get married! It is imperative that both of you receive counsel at the same time. If not, you are already headed for destruction in your relationship due to separateness' influence.

There are too many men and women using the following phrase: *"This is **MY** money. I bought this with **MY** money."* The money you or she makes is for the family and operation of your home, not to be given to some silly man or woman "in the street" (that silly person could very well be a relative or friend). Speaking in terms of "MY" allows division to enter the home and can open the door for poverty and deception to roost while setting your family up with a dysfunctional spirit. As spouses, you must come on one accord to determine how the family's finances are spent.

Hiding money from the other in a separate bank account is not optional. If your spouse misuses the money in any way, seek God for guidance. Now, it's okay to have different accounts if you're not hiding anything from one another. It's all about the intent. Remember what I've repeatedly said: The devil is always looking for ways to enter your relationship. Don't allow finances to be one of those ways!

The wife is subject to the husband in all things, as long as he follows Christ. Following are some examples of him **NOT** following Christ:

- If your husband degrades, embarrasses, or humiliates you by beating you up or cussing you out in front of people, he's **NOT** following Christ.
- If he tells you to steal, sell your body, or wants to participate in wife-swapping/swinging, he's **NOT** following Christ.

➢ If he instructs you to sell drugs or anything else that goes against the will of God, he's **NOT** following Christ.
➢ If he wants you to go along with his lying and cheating, he's **NOT** following Christ.

Many men have never learned how to properly and respectfully talk to their wife or woman. They dictate to them instead of talking. They abuse and misuse instead of communicating with God first and then with their significant other. There are too many men involved in this type of abusive lifestyle. Men, if this is you, you must put that controlling spirit to rest. Please do not raise your children in this manner. None of those ingredients reflect the character of God. You are encouraged to go before God and ask Him what to do. Do not lean on your own understanding (read Proverbs 3:5-7). Repent and be a positive role model in your family's life.

REMEMBER: You must **LIVE BY EXAMPLE**, according to the Word of God.

If you have a wife, it is your responsibility to cultivate her into becoming what God has called her to be, the wife she was chosen to be, and the mother she needs to be. If **YOU** try to "make" your spouse into what you want, they will never become who and what you genuinely need them to be.

When you enter into a relationship or marriage where children are involved, they may resent you and feel as if you're trying to take the place of the absent parent or even remove them from the parent's life. You are viewed as an intruder. This is a plot of the devil against the marriage and family to bring forth division in the home. The devil will do anything and everything he can to cause confusion, division, or divorce. It's his job—and he does it well.

This devastating blow to marriage can develop from the lack of knowledge of God, not knowing God, not knowing who you are in Christ, and not applying the Word of God in your life, home, family, and marriage, especially in the area of communicating with each other and God. Much understanding is needed, as well as patience and a humble spirit.

What you have to remember is that sometimes, the child may resent being corrected by the parent(s). In some cases, they become evasive and operate under a spirit of denial or rebellion. In situations like this, going before God in prayer and learning the best way to handle discipline is needed.

WARNING: DO NOT WAIT UNTIL THE CHILD BEGINS TO BE RUDE BEFORE TRYING TO EFFECT CHANGE!!!

Men, some girls may humbly accept you, especially when she's at the age when she needs a father's guidance. However, be careful; don't rush the relationship with her, as this can cause her to see you in a different light. Be mindful of how you show her fatherly affection because as her young mind develops, she can misconstrue that affection as romanticism. Guard your mind and pray for her heart as you both transition into the newness of the father/daughter relationship.

Has there ever been a time (during or after sex) when you've heard a woman say, *"I love you!"* or *"I want to have your baby!"?* Some men will use those words as a tool to play on her feelings and use them for his own selfish gain. What the woman doesn't realize is that she is operating under the guise of a seducing spirit as well as a spirit of confusion. At the time, her spirit and body received the man as one (just as a husband and wife are one). Her body and desires receive him as if he was her husband, and she gives herself to him out of tainted love disguised as false love and lust. After sex has stimulated her body, it is only natural for her to feel "love" because that is how her body and desire to know him are received. Sometimes, she may not be aware that she even uttered those words.

Gentlemen, you have just violated the temple of the Holy Spirit and committed adultery against God!

A very disgusting reality is that there are a lot of men and women sleeping with their children. Put that spirit to rest; no more incest!

Most men are very protective over their daughters. You don't want any boy or man violating her but at the same time, if your son goes out there and "gets a little bit," you stick your chest out and say, *"My boy is now a man!"* That protective nature you have over your daughter is the same you should have about your son, girlfriend, or future wife.

REMEMBER: Your girlfriend or future wife
is someone's daughter, too!

Men, we must learn how to discipline ourselves in all situations. Let's stop these disrespectful behaviors. Break the chain, be a man, and take a stand. I know you can do it! It is of the utmost urgency. We, as men, must regularly read, study, and stay rooted in the Word of the **ALMIGHTY GOD.**

In all things, there must be a well-defined structure in the home that utilizes the authority of the husband and the influence and nurturing of the wife. All men are called to cultivate their wives and daughters, developing them into respectable women. They must be shown that their father, dad, boyfriend, and husband have their best interests at heart.

Men, avoid using harsh words and phrases at all times. Remember that the words you say carry a lasting impact and impression on children and adults (read Proverbs 18:20; Mark 11:23). The best way to understand how well you communicate or discipline others is how you respond when you are angry, tired, or sick. When you respond humbly — in meekness — under any of those conditions, **THAT** is real discipline.

REMEMBER: Disciplining also comes in the form of an attitude adjustment.

There are five steps we can follow in helping to train our children:

1. We must teach them how to survive, which includes proper eating habits, physical and oral hygiene, educating them on how to make wise decisions, and applying the Word of God in every area of their lives.
2. You can begin teaching your children the difference between good and evil, as well as the difference between right and wrong. This process should begin before birth (that's right; before they are born). They must be taught

how important it is for them to obey their parents, for this is the first commandment and comes with a promise of a long life.

Since the beginning, from when Adam and Eve ate from the Tree of Knowledge of Good and Evil, everyone born into this world is born with the same knowledge (read Genesis 2:17). I implore you not to wait for a child to be born with their sin nature, but to speak to their spirit while in the mother's womb.

3. Ask yourself: Who has the most influence on the family as it relates to giving wise counsel? To be a good example, you must first be a good follower and partaker in the things that are of God.

So, let me ask you this: When do you believe is the right time to talk to your children about sex? Here are some helpful answers:

- ➢ Ask God to reveal to you the right time and age, as well as giving you spiritual insight into this matter.
- ➢ God may tell you to begin before you see your little girl developing into a young lady or when she becomes interested in boys.
- ➢ You may be directed to begin before your son becomes interested in having a girlfriend or when he's no longer too shy to ask a girl out on a date.

Don't let them hear about sex from a friend or in the streets first. Tell them right away: No sex before marriage. Read what the Word says concerning fornication and other sexual matters, making it clear how sin affects the body.

4. Men, if you are married and operating in the position of daddy, talk to your daughter about sex under the guidance of the Holy Spirit. Tell her about the tricks that boys play to get them into bed, what to watch for, and what to listen out for in their conversations.
5. Women, if you are married and operating in the position of mommy, talk to your son about sex under the guidance of the Holy Spirit. Tell him what girls are looking for in a young man and what she needs to help her grow into a beautiful and respectful woman.

NOTE: In either of the above scenarios, you can even make a list that can be used for a guideline.

Don't be so quick to follow in someone else's footsteps. After all, you don't know what they had to do to get to where they are! It could have been sex with the boss. It could have involved theft and deceit. It could be that they were forced to have sex with a same-sex partner. Choosing to mimic another's lifestyle can cause you to suffer from an identity crisis (a double-minded spirit).

If you have been sexually active with multiple partners, you may not have acquired a Sexually-Transmitted Disease; however, how many spirits have you picked up or left behind? How many people have YOU infected?

REMEMBER: If you don't mind living that kind of lifestyle,
then you have no respect for yourself
and are choosing to live immorally.

Minister Aaron Weaver

You must first learn to love yourself. If you don't, how will you know how to love someone else? Take a moment to read Proverbs 16:23. I'll wait…

Then, read John 15:7. I'll wait…

Through discipline given with love, you **WILL** get the victory!

A Prayer of Discipline

Father, in the Name of Jesus:

Help me to become a man of discipline in all my ways, for the road of discipline is the gateway to manhood.

Jesus, guide me and direct me on what I need to do to walk in an upright manner in all things; my marriage, eating habits, spending money, working, training, raising my children, and studying Your Word to show myself faithful.

Father, help me realize that I must first discipline my spirit and have a renewed mind. Only then will the body follow.

In Jesus' Name, I pray,

Amen.

CHAPTER 4

PRIDE AND SELFISHNESS

I Once Was Blind, But Now I See

Pride is a subtle and destructive spirit. Often, we're not aware of the effects it can have on us. It's like a disease that runs rampant in the land. There is no cure. There is no vaccination known to man that can help. Pride thrives off of our emotions and enhances our ego, to the point where we choose not to hear or are blinded and deafened to the truth.

Pride doesn't just enter into a man's heart all at once. It rolls in like the morning fog, slowly creeping across the water and before you know it, it has engulfed you in the mist of immaturity.

REMEMBER: This state of immaturity will cloud your judgment and increase your anger. It will make you suspicious for no reason at all and bombard your life with spirits of jealousy, bitterness, and frustration.

Pride will bring you to a state of total defeat and destruction, or it will bring you to your knees before God (the choice is yours).

This spirit has been in existence since before the beginning of time. It first began with Lucifer, the fallen angel (aka Satan). When operating in the spirit of pride, we hide behind the false wall of our masculinity and act immaturely. There's no room for growth when pride steps in.

Before we can take dominion over the earth and before we can rule our house well, we must first learn how to be a good follower (see Genesis 1:26). Don't get so wrapped up in your purpose as a man, husband, father, or dad to the point that you're not willing to learn.

Just think:

- Noah had to **learn** how to build an ark before he could save himself and his family from the flood.
- Moses had to **learn** how to take care of a herd of sheep before God Almighty could trust him to lead the people out of Egypt.
- David had to **learn** how to face his fears as well as tend to and protect the sheep before he killed a giant.

How can we protect and care for our family if we don't first learn the importance of becoming a husband and leader?

REMEMBER: God is our Provider and through Him, He gives us the provisions to provide for our family.

Please rid yourself of the spirit of denial and take the blame for your actions.

Pride isn't all bad, though. It does have its good points. We can (for example) take pride in keeping our homes neat and clean, performing our jobs with excellence, and in our appearance and personal hygiene.

Which one will you choose?

- Pride — arrogance, controlling, immaturity.
- Pride — wisdom, growth, prosperity, and productive.

Once again, the choice is up to you!

Selfishness

I call selfishness the "blood brother of pride." They are closely-related and almost inseparable. In many cases, they work hand-in-hand. Scripture tells us that iniquity (immorality) was found in Lucifer's heart (the place where pride and selfishness are formed).

The spirit of selfishness was passed down through the bloodline of Adam. It, too, runs rampant in the world today and brings with it an uncontrollable urge to get everything it can all for itself...with the spirit of greed following closely behind.

Take, for example, if you steal something from someone or flirt with someone else's spouse or significant other, you are operating under the spirit of selfishness because you are coveting something that or someone who does not belong to you.

Another act of selfishness is called a "crab mentality." This happens when someone pulls another back down with them, in essence keeping them in poverty.

This curse is influenced by spirits of jealousy, low self-esteem, a vengeful heart, bitterness, and greed. Sadly, it can sometimes occur in your home or with a family member (read part of Abram's story in Genesis 12:1-4).

Greed

Greed is not concerned or worried about whether or not you have enough for yourself or your family; it just wants what you have! The more you feed greed, the more it wants from you. It will never have enough—and when you cannot supply its needs, it will go somewhere else to get it!

Greed most often shows up in our children, family members, or friends. They want what you have or what you can give them; **BUT** when it comes time for them to reciprocate, they are nowhere to be found.

REMEMBER: Greed is the sister of pride and selfishness. She's just like a leech: a taker, not a giver.

When we work together and support one another, we can become very successful. How do you think those in corporate America have become a success? Easy: They work together as one!

Don't take your anger out on each other (we wrestle not against flesh and blood). Instead, put it to work to develop yourselves into what God has ordained for you to be. Expose the devil for the **LIAR** that he is and put these spirits of lack and poverty behind you. Put the bitterness aside, live for God, and be victorious!

If no one reaches out to help you in your time of need, give it to God. He will lead you to the right person or send someone to you. Remember always to pray first so that you can discern who it is that God sent!

I Once Was Blind, But Now I See

A Prayer of Forgiveness

My Heavenly Father:

I have let pride, greed, and selfishness plague my life and caused the blessings of Abraham to pass me by. Forgive me, restore me, and deliver me from operating under the influence of these spirits.

In the Name of Jesus, pride, greed, and selfishness have no place in my life anymore. I bind these spirits from operating in my life. I cancel your assignments from off of my family and me, for the Word of God says in Isaiah 54:17, *"No weapon formed against me shall prosper"* and in Mark 3:35, *"He who does the will of My Father is m brother, sister, and mother."*

It is written in Ezekiel 36:26 that You, Heavenly Father, will take away the stony heart and give us a heart of flesh. Therefore, in the Name of Jesus, I release the spirits of love, the peace of God, self-control, humility, honesty, and respect for one another as well as myself.

Thank you, Jesus, for I am now free.

Amen.

CHAPTER 5

TRADITIONS AND HOLIDAYS

I Once Was Blind, But Now I See

The Word of God says that the traditions of man make His Word ineffective. For example, when our children lie to us, we get angry, discipline them, and take away their privileges. However, in the same breath, we have taught our children traditions passed down to us that were based on lies.

REMEMBER: Tradition is one of the seven things that are an abomination unto the Lord (read Proverbs 6:16-19).

A "traditional" biblical account that is often misconstrued is the tale of the three wise men finding Jesus in the manger. That is not true. In the Book of Matthew 2:1, it reads, *"Now, when Jesus was born in Bethlehem of Judea in the days of Herod, the king, behold, there came wise men [not THREE of them]."* In verse nine, the Word says, *"The star went before them, and stood over the place where the YOUNG CHILD was [not a BABY]."* In the tenth verse, Scripture states He was found in a **HOUSE** with his mother, Mary—not in a manger.

We must be mindful to rightly divide God's Word of Truth.

Jesus was two years old when they found Him. Don't forget the **WHOLE** of the story: King Herod ordered all of the children up to the age of two killed, hoping that Jesus was among them who were slain.

Now, venture your way to Luke 2:8. Therein, you will find that the **SHEPHERDS** were the ones who found Jesus in the manger. On that night, there were three different signs:

1. The first sign was that a virgin gave birth to a baby boy (the Messiah).
2. The second sign was when an angel appeared to the **SHEPHERDS** in a field as they were watching their sheep. The angel told them that they would find the baby in a manger, wrapped in swaddling clothes (milk rags).
3. The third sign was the multitude of angels that filled the sky, singing praises to celebrate the birth of Immanuel (Jesus; God is with us).

Christmas

Some religions do not celebrate Christmas, even though we know that the 25th of December is not the birthdate of Jesus. In fact, some religions don't celebrate any holidays whatsoever, but in the Book of Luke 2:14-15, it states that the angels sang praises to God (Elohim) and filled the heavens with their presence at the birth of Jesus.

If you can't celebrate His birth, why, then, did the angels do it?

Christmas is the day we are supposed to celebrate the birth of unselfish love, for it was Jesus who took away the sins of the world and received the world unto Himself. This gift (Jesus) took 30 years of preparation while He was on this earth, with an additional three more years to fulfill His purpose.

*"For Jesus is the way, truth, and the life;
no man comes to the Father but by Him"* (John 14:6).

I Once Was Blind, But Now I See

REMEMBER: No matter what anyone tells you, **JESUS** is the only way for your salvation and eternal life in Heaven. Jesus is the reason for the Christmas season
(in fact, He's the reason for **EVERY** season)!

Let me tell you what Christmas is **NOT**: It is **NOT** a man dressed in a red and white suit with a black belt and black boots hopping from chimney to chimney giving away toys.

The Holy Spirit gave it to me this way: The white represents the purity of Jesus. The red represents the blood that was shed to redeem us from our sins. The joy that is received from the laughter we hear is the joy of the Lord that gives us strength and heals the spirit, soul, and body. The black belt is to strap you with the truth. The black boots represent the transition from our old walk of life into our new walk in the Word (Jesus and everlasting life). *"For God so loved the world, that He gave His Only Begotten Son..."* (read John 3:16-18).

God shows us His love every day. Our salvation is a daily walk. One moment, you're here; the next, you're not.

Even now, as I sit and meditate on the goodness of God on what to write next, the Holy Spirit is saying to me:

"It is good to remember the day Jesus was born, but there's another thing that happened as well. A man named Joseph took a young maiden (who was a virgin) to be his wife. He endured persecution and had to practice self-control. Joseph also prevented shame from coming upon Mary, for she would have been stoned for having a baby out of wedlock. Joseph demonstrated an act of a father's

unselfish love and provided comfort and security to protect Mary and be obedient to the voice of God."

Another thing the Holy Spirit is telling me is that Jesus was a virgin in two ways:

1. He never knew a woman—neither in the physical nor in His heart.
2. He had no known sin. He was innocent to sin (a virgin), yet He became a sin offering for us.

Thanksgiving

"One Horse, Open Sleigh" (better known as Jingle Bells) is associated with the Christmas season but was actually written for Thanksgiving.

John Hanson declared that the 4th Thursday of every November is Thanksgiving Day.

If you can't give thanks to God for who He is and for what He has done for you and your family, then something is wrong with you **and** your religion.

New Year's Eve

New Year's Eve is a very important day for many people. Some say that if you don't have a man or woman when the New Year starts, you will be alone for the rest of the year. Tell me this: Why would you allow someone to speak a curse over you? Use the time alone to get yourself together. Stop being insecure. Get rid of the low self-esteem and show **YOURSELF** some love and appreciation.

Many people use this and other holidays to fall into a state of depression. Don't let this happen to you, especially when it comes to drinking and driving or overindulging. That is an act of selfishness, immaturity, and insecurity. Let the New Year's holiday be a new beginning for you.

REMEMBER: Getting drunk or using drugs does not make the pain go away, neither does it change your situation. Doing these things slowly destroys you. If you keep it up, you may never see your loved ones in Heaven because Heaven may not be your next eternal home. Please, in Jesus' Name: Don't leave that legacy behind for your children to remember you by.

There's nothing wrong with watching the clock and counting down the last minutes of the old year as it brings in the new. Furthermore, there's nothing wrong with watching the fireworks light up the night sky. Try this: The next time you view fireworks, look at them with spiritual eyes, and you will see the manifestation of Spiritual Warfare in process. Every demonic spirit that thought it had you in the prior year is under attack and has been destroyed. Don't let them return. Keep them dead in your and your family's life in the New Year.

Weddings

What about celebrating weddings? Jesus (as The Word) went to Adam and Eve, and God performed the first wedding! Celebrate the union of man and woman to the fullest!

Father's Day

In the Roman Catholic tradition, Father's Day is celebrated on Saint Joseph's Day which is on the 19th of March. In New Orleans, Louisiana, it is the day when those who masquerade as Indians have a contest to see who will win for the best or original costume.

Mardi Gras / Fat Tuesday / Carnival

In New Orleans, Louisiana, Mardi Gras is a popular and well-celebrated time of year—a time when the whole city practically shuts down. People come from all over the world to party and have a good time.

However, most are not aware that they are synonymously worshiping false gods (this tradition goes on in other cities and countries as well).

Following are a few of the names "celebrated" during the holiday:

- **Zeus:** The god of thunder.
- **Pegasus:** A mythical, flying horse.
- **Cleopatra:** She operated under the spirits of suicide and lust.
- **Neptune:** He was called the 'King of the Sea.'

Whey party-goers raise their hands in celebration, what they're doing is giving honor and praise to these and other false gods. The trinkets (such as the beads and coins) that are tossed represent the jewelry and money the gods are giving to their subjects. The girls in the front of the band represent the dancers of seduction praising their false gods.

REMEMBER: These are the things that are happening in real-time in the spirit realm of demonic forces. This is Satan's method of going into battle against you to deceive you and bring death, hell, and destruction into your life. Anything and everything the devil can do to arouse your flesh, he will do.

Now, I'm not calling your or your children idol worshipers. However, when we see things in the spirit realm, we should write them down, tell someone, and address it immediately.

Let me demonstrate how the enemy has changed things to deceive people:

- In the Holy Bible, God had the praise dancers go first before every battle. They were followed by the drummers, as the roar of thunder filled the air to announce they were coming. The warriors then showed up on the scene last.

During Mardi Gras celebrations, people get comfortable with others "like them." In every city, state, and country that participates in the festivities, there is a territorial demon in charge. His job is to keep sin active in his territory.

Do you remember the biblical account of the cities of Sodom and Gomorrah? Their wickedness was so great, God obliterated them. A little-known fact is that the destruction was also to include the city of Zoar, but Lot asked the angel to spare it and to send him there instead of to the mountains (read Genesis 19:16-21), but Lot later changed his mind and went to the mountains (see Genesis 19:30).

From the word "carnival" comes the word "carnivorous," which means meat or flesh-eater. No matter where you go to celebrate, be aware of their customs, traditions, and festivals (some call it carnival; others call it festival).

Although New Orleans, Louisiana is known to be a party city, there's so much more. With its beautiful landscapes, the French Quarters, Saint Charles Avenue, Saint Louis Cathedral, the Steam Boat, and yes, even Bourbon Street, the city gives you a warm, southern spirit of hospitality, welcome, and love.

Many people say that New Orleans is "The City that Care Forgot." I'm here to tell you: God is changing it to "The City that Cares!" Out of every city or state I've ever lived or visited, there is no place like New Orleans. I love it! It is the place of my birth, and I wouldn't trade it for any other city or country in the world.

Resurrection Day (Easter)

This is the time when we celebrate the resurrection of our Lord Jesus the Christ from the grave. His death represents the sins of the world, brought to Hell and left there. Because of His death, we are dead to sin, sickness, disease, and poverty. His resurrection represents our transition from death to eternal life.

I Once Was Blind, But Now I See

REMEMBER: He that is in Christ is a new creature. Old things are passed away; behold, all things become new.

Easter and Christmas are often the only Sundays people go to church. Most often, they go to show off their new clothes, receive a gift, or get something else for free. Don't let any of those "reasons" be yours. God is not concerned about your new clothes, gifts, or any other material thing. He wants to know where your heart is (read Matthew 6:33). Whenever you attend church, let it be to serve God. Have no other agenda.

The Easter Bunny

The symbol of the Easter Bunny originated with the pagan festival of Easter. The goddess, Ishtar, was worshipped by the Anglo-Saxons through her earthly symbol: the rabbit. The Germans brought the symbol of the Easter rabbit to America.

It was widely ignored in Christianity until shortly after the Civil War. In many churches, the resurrection of Jesus takes a backseat to Easter baskets, the bunny, and candy. Sitting in the forefront is the celebration of the "Spring season" through Ishtar. Another goddess connected with the holiday is Ashtart—the goddess of fertility, sexuality, and war—commonly-known as Aphrodite and Diana.

The Decorated Easter Egg

The egg is sometimes called "Nature's Perfect Package." It has been used for magic, medicine, food, and omens. In pagan times, the egg represented the rebirth of the earth:

Winter was over, and a new life began. The egg was believed to have special powers and was sometimes buried under the foundation of buildings to ward off evil. Pregnant young Roman women carried an egg on their persons to foretell the sex of their unborn children. French brides stepped on an egg before crossing the threshold of their new home.

There's an old legend **(MYTH)** that states Mary (the mother of Jesus) gave some eggs to the soldiers at the cross and, as Mary cried, her tears fell upon the eggs, causing them to sparkle with a beautiful array of colors.

One Polish legend states that when Mary Magdalene went to the tomb to anoint the body of Jesus, she had with her a basket of eggs to serve as a repast. When she arrived and uncovered the eggs, the pure white shells had miraculously taken on a rainbow of colors.

Decorating and coloring eggs for Easter was the custom in England during the Middle Ages.

The first Faberge egg was an egg within an egg. It had an outside shell of platinum (an enameled white shell) that opened to reveal a smaller gold egg. The smaller egg, in turn, opened to display a golden chicken and a jeweled replica of the Imperial Crown.

40 Days of Length

There is a legend about a woman whose son was missing. She thought he was dead. She was told to go on a 40-day fast, and her son would then return. After the 40 days had passed, her son returned. To celebrate, they exchanged eggs. This was to celebrate what they referred to as her son's resurrection from the dead.

I had a brother-in-Christ tell me that he was giving up something for Length. At that point, God immediately placed in my spirit the tradition of man's way of doing things. This is another tradition of man that makes God's Word ineffective.

People of God: **STOP** putting sin to the side for Length and get rid of it for **GOOD**!

God said to me, *"Instead of giving up something of the world for 40 days, pull down something from Heaven that's of Me and operate in it for 40 days so that My will can be manifested here on earth as it is in Heaven"* (read Matthew 6:10).

Once and for all, kick away the tradition of man and don your feet with the gospel of grace. Use it as a lamp to guide your out of the bondage of "tradition."

Halloween

Halloween is the worst traditional day of all. It is the day when death, Hell, and destruction are recognized on earth.

At one time, practically all of us masqueraded as demonic spirits along with our siblings, friends, and other family members. We were disguised as witches, ghosts, monsters, and a host of other evil creatures.

There are some who decorate their homes and businesses and filling them with weird noises and terrifying sounds to represent the evil of the holiday. What we don't realize is that we have given a pathway to every demonic force to enter that space or become attached to those in its wake.

Halloween is the night of "All Hollow's Eve" when witches and occults operate and prey upon unsuspecting people, innocent children, and even animals. In some cases, people are sacrificed, the drinking of their warm blood is customary, and the victim's raw heart is consumed (eaten). *"Ye shall not eat anything with the blood; neither shall ye use enchantment nor observe times"* (Leviticus 19:2).

It's been said that witches are known to be seen with black cats. The reason for that is because familiar spirits were known to possess black cats. The cats were used for guidance and instruction. Witches have also been known to use frogs, toads, owls, or any other small animal of their choosing.

DID YOU KNOW? Watching horror movies on television can release demonic spirits into your home where they take up residence. They may even linger and attach themselves to you, your family, and objects in your home. This could very well be one of the reasons why there is no peace in your home or life.

If you or someone in your home play vulgar music or watches R-rated or X-rated movies (under the guise of 'entertainment'), those spirits have already taken up residence. Many spirits travel through the airwaves into your home.

REMEMBER: When you or someone else in your home watch vulgar television shows or perverted movies, you have given the spirit of abuse a welcome mat into your home life, which will cause you to operate in the works of the flesh (read Galatians 5:19-21). The exposure to those spirits may not affect you immediately, but they can in the future by surfacing in your children, grandchildren, or great-grandchildren. The best thing to do is pray over and anoint yourself and family daily.

Many people have fallen into the trap of the enemy (the devil) while thinking there's nothing wrong with participating in "fun" activities. These things are a highway to your soul, your home, your children, and their children. Shut the door to the demonic world **TODAY**!

Horoscope and Zodiac Signs

There are those who use the signs of the Zodiac for enchantment, magic, incantations, spells, charms, and even a means of identification (i.e., *"I'm a Leo, and Leos always do such-and-such"*). Spirits work through the spirit of deception.

I won't address **ALL** the signs of the Zodiac here; just the ones the Holy Spirit is leading me to mention:

- **Libra**—You are not a scale. Your life is unbalanced because of the personal, physical, and financial decisions you've made. Everyone has experienced some form of ups and downs in their life. Without God, you will never have a balanced life.

- **Cancer** — You are not a crab; neither are you a deadly disease that feeds off a person's living body until they die.
- **Scorpio** — You are not a scorpion. The scorpion represents death. Where is grave's victory? Oh, death: Where is your sting?
- **Pisces** — You are not a fish going around and around in circles. This is a spirit of confusion.
- **Sagittarius** — You are not a half-man/half-horse mutant. You were made in the image and likeness of God (see Genesis 1:26).
- **Leo** — The sign for Leo is a lion. Satan goes around like a roaring lion, hunting down his prey to devour them. The devil is a counterfeit lion and a coward. **THE LION** (note the difference in comparison) represents Jesus. Jesus is the King of Kings and the Lord of Lords.
- **Capricorn** — If you associate yourself with a goat and your children are running around like a bunch of wild animals, then what do you expect? A "kid" is a young goat. The word "kid" can be used by the enemy any way he pleases.
  - *Pam* — There was a mythical creature called Pam. This beast was half-man/half-goat. He played his enchanted flute to seduce women and to hypnotize them with his music (to sleep with a creature is against the will of God). Some people have sex with dogs, sheep, and other wild animals.
- **Aries** — In the Greek, Aries is the name of the red planet: Mars. At one time, Mars was called the "Angry Red Planet" and the "Planet of War."

I Once Was Blind, But Now I See

Those were just a few signs to be mindful of. Don't associate yourself with them, as you could find yourself entangled in their webs. Don't let them rule your life or dictate to you how to live, where to go, or who to marry. We live by the examples of Jesus Christ, not by Zodiac signs.

Please stay away from fortune-tellers, palm readers, and hypnotists. Those methods probe the mind by using the spirit of divination, which can open the path for familiar spirits to embody you (read Deuteronomy 18:11; Isaiah 19:3). One of the things they will tell you is that at some time in the past, you had another life. How is that possible when the dead cannot communicate with the living?

When a medium talks to a spirit or has a séance and you are told it is a "good spirit," that is not true. **ANY** spirit either of you communicates with is evil. Anyone who performs those types of rituals is talking to a demonic or familiar spirit. The "voice" of spirits emanating through another is not God's way of communicating with your or His people. Don't fall for it!

BE AWARE: Some mediums may try to harm you. Others will even offer you advice (don't take it). Quite often, the person is a **FAKE**!

If you are aware that a house is haunted or you have seen movies about someone's ghost roaming around from hundreds of years ago, all of these images are territorial spirits — demons that have been assigned to a specific space, place, or territory. Remember always that these spirits are not your family member or friend who has since passed away.

Once again, I remind you that those spirits come to deceive you. They want you to believe and trust in them. However, the **ONLY** good spirit is the **HOLY SPIRIT**! Please let everyone you know how important it is to their life and the welfare of their household to kill this foolishness once and for all.

If you are trapped in this maze of horror, pray the following prayer. Ask God to forgive you and deliver you from its grasp.

A Prayer of Repentance

Heavenly Father:

Forgive me for trusting in people, a rabbit's foot, four-leaf clovers, horseshoes, so-called lucky numbers, symbols, my horoscope, fortune-tellers, and any other inanimate object to guide me through my life.

Forgive me, Father, for operating under a spirit of idolatry.

I repent this day and surrender my will and my life over to you.

I accept you, Jesus, as my Lord and personal Savior.

Sweet, Holy Spirit: Come into my heart and guide me in all things, for You are my Counselor, Guide, and Teacher.

In Jesus' Name,

Amen.

CHAPTER 6

THE WOMAN IN AUTHORITY

Dysfunctional and Controlling

In this day and age, some women don't want to get married. They feel they can do it all by themselves. If she was to be honest with herself, she is undergoing an identity crisis. Why? Because it is **IMPOSSIBLE** to function as both the man and woman.

Men, God did not design a woman to operate in both positions. If the loving and nurturing part of her rules, then the children may run all over her. If she rules like "a man," she can be too firm or controlling.

What happens is that the woman experiences the effects of a double-minded spirit, pulling her in two different directions. The spirits of confusion, anger, and frustration have now taken up camp. This can be very dangerous and force the woman to become very defensive.

However, there are some women—both single and married—that have a spirit of intimidation, as well as an arrogant spirit. They refuse to submit (be under a man's authority or leadership) because they feel no man can live up to their standards or expectations. Why is that so? Because their standards are of a Jezebel spirit.

Ladies, the only standard you should expect a man to live up to is **GOD'S** standard and way of doing things (see Matthew 6:33). From the beginning, pay attention to how he treats his mother, sister, and other women, as well as how he treats you. Ask yourself: Is he a good model of a God-fearing man? Now, don't expect your man to be perfect. After all, you're not perfect. If you do what must be done as a woman of God and let God work within him, both of you will experience the joy of the Lord in your lives!

Don't be so focused on being independent that you don't see the man God has placed in your life to cover and protect you — the man who will help you reach your goals, fulfill your purpose, and support you all the way (as well as being a dad to the children). A man who wants to be with you just for sex is not Godsent. You should pray for a man who loves you for the woman of God and lady he sees inside of you.

To the gentlemen: Be careful. Some women may have entered into a stage of entanglement — a controlling web that is laced with a non-submissive spirit. Let God show you how to cultivate the woman who loves you and desires to be more to you than just a piece of meat. It is likely that deep within, she is crying out to become a true "lady," and you can be just the catalyst she needs to have that vision come to fruition.

Men, when you move into a woman's home, you feed the spirit of witchcraft even more. What you have done is given her the authoritative role and placed her in the position as the head of the household. She gets to call the shots. She gets to make the decisions on what she will and will not accept in **HER** house. So, you have to make a choice: Will you stay? Do you wish to succumb to that controlling spirit?

REMEMBER: I stated before that the minute you moved in together outside of marriage, the home became dysfunctional. If you love each other, get married before you begin living together!

Deception

The spirit of deception often grabs a stronghold in a woman early in her life through unwise counsel, poor advice, rejection, and the desire to be accepted. This can instill in her a spirit of low self-esteem or an overcompensating sense of independence. As such, when the relationship begins, she may say things to you like, *"Don't get too serious. We're just friends. I'm not looking for a commitment."*

When a woman who's independent gets involved in a relationship or gets married (whether children are a factor or not), you will encounter a lot of friction in your relationship that neither of you has experienced before. Why? Because God must strip away those things of your past that can or will hinder you from reaching the destination He has ordained for both of you.

REMEMBER: The more you complain or grumble, the longer you will go through the affliction (wilderness).

Men, a woman who is independent will not put up with or tolerate a weak man who will not take a stand in a relationship or marriage. Examples of a man being "weak" include him saying things such as:

- *"Whatever you say, dear."*
- *"Wherever you want to go is fine with me."*
- *"I don't have the time. You take care of it."*
- *"Since you're working a full-time job, I'll stay home with the children."*
- *"Baby, there's no work out there for me."*
- *"That job isn't paying enough."*

When it comes time to discipline the children, you let her decide the punishment and how long it should last. Then, when you implement one form of discipline, she changes it — sometimes right in front of you — and you don't say anything at all.

To make it plain, the woman treats the man like a child. She's the mother and authority figure in the home because there's no role model of a man of God to guide her.

Leadership and Authority

When Eve listened to the serpent in the Garden of Eden, God cursed the serpent by taking away his legs. The serpent (which is now a snake) was left to crawl on his belly forever (see Genesis 3:12-24). The serpent wasn't the only one to suffer the consequences of deception and disobedience.

Scripture tells us that the sorrow of the woman was multiplied in conception, during pregnancy, and in labor with contractions. In Adam's case, the ground was cursed from whence he came. He had to farm what turned into a land fraught with thorns and stickers, and he did so with sweat forming on his forehead.

Here's the message here: Because Adam submitted to his wife in the Garden, a spirit of division has taken place in the "home" and continues to spread to all mankind. The authority of leadership was given to man by God but was lost — given up by Adam — by a passive spirit through disobedience. How?

- He didn't take his rightful place to stop his wife and the serpent from speaking to one another.
- He knew that specific tree was off-limits.
- He gave in to his wife's request to take part in eating the forbidden fruit, knowing full well it was against God's command.
- After blaming God for what happened, **THEN** he confessed to what he did (read Genesis 2:16-17; 3:17-19).

It's important to note here that the woman was not called "Eve" until **AFTER** Adam ate of the fruit (see Genesis 3:20).

Ladies, please read Genesis 3:17 and learn why it's difficult for [some] men to take orders (instructions) from a woman.

Men, let's be honest here: Sometimes, we have a hard time taking instruction from a woman in authority. Whether it's your wife, mother, or boss, don't look at it as "taking orders from a woman." Instead, humble yourself under the authority she operates under. It's highly probable that she's acting under the authority God has given her, with the purpose of humbling **YOU** while helping you become the man of God and leader God is preparing you to be!

REMEMBER: Cussing or raising your voice will only keep you on the potter's wheel longer.

Men, sometimes a woman (wife, mother, sister, or even a boss) can overstep her authority. When that happens, the lion in you must rise with meekness (power under control). You must listen to how God wants you to respond to that situation. Take the time to learn how to be a humble servant.

REMEMBER: You cannot become a good leader unless you first become a good follower. If you don't wish to follow, then you will never know or learn how to be a wise leader.

Men, a woman wants a man who is going to lead her and the family, not a man who wants to be led by her. For example, one of the reasons you should have a job is to prepare you to be a leader. You must learn how to follow instructions and operate under a spirit of submission to get the job done and endure all the mess that comes along with it as well (don't forget to pray, pray, pray while you're going through the situation).

Humble Women in Authority

God has used many women throughout the Bible to have His will done.

- God used Esther to save her people. She took it upon herself to go before the kind without his permission. For that act, she could have been beheaded.
- Deborah was a prophet and a judge. She was a mighty warrior. There was a time when some soldiers wouldn't even go into battle without her!
- Mary (mother of Jesus) submitted to the will of God to birth His Son.

Those are just a few of the women God used to take a position of leadership or who made a bold stand for His will,

His Word, and His way. In fact, many women are sensitive to the voice of God—likely more than you think.

DID YOU KNOW? When Christ appeared in the Upper Room, women were there as well. They, too, received the Holy Spirit (read Acts 1:14-15).

The ignorance of man chooses not to study or learn the Word and cannot rightly-divide it. The stupidity of man's ignorance says that a woman can't preach the Word of God in the pulpit, on the altar, or on a stage. That foolish thinking is simply untrue. Women who love God and have been anointed and appointed by God can function in the church as well as in other areas of ministry.

Think about it: There are many women in politics or in control of large corporations. Why? Is it because they have more wisdom, are more dedicated, or because they are well-organized? Maybe so, for God has no respect of person. He [God] chooses whomever He wills, whether it be a man, woman, or child.

Men, rid yourself of the spirit of fear and intimidation by women. If you are intimidated by a woman, just imagine what will happen if God used your wife, daughter, mother, or another woman instead of choosing you!

What Brought You Together?

Men, there is something I would like to remind you about and bring to your attention as I close this chapter:

If you are staying in a house with a woman and you're not married to her, you have no authority in that house; you are trespassing. No matter how you spin it, that is **NOT** your castle (home). You have defiled her home and are misleading the children. Although you may be helping, teaching, and supporting them, you are destroying them spiritually and morally. If you are living together, take your relationship before the Lord and let Him guide you.

To both the men and women: If you're sexually-involved and the other does not want to get married, most likely they never will. The best thing for you to do is leave them alone. Don't listen to the tired lies of the enemy:

- *"Let's just live together for a while."*
- *"If we move in together, we can save money."*
- *"We'll get married after the baby is born."*
- *"We'll get married after you get a better job."*
- *"I love you, but I'm not ready to get married."*
- *"I don't want to be tied down."*
- *"I love you — but not like THAT."*

REMEMBER: Don't compromise with the devil.
If you keep playing with fire, you will get burned.

If you desire to get married, take a careful look at what you see. Are you sure you are willing to put up with and endure each other's issues? Be mindful that it will take time, patience, and a devoted relationship both before and in the marriage — ashes to ashes, dust to dust.

I Once Was Blind, But Now I See

Some women in authority will not easily relinquish their independence. If she is a working woman in a career, she may feel she has too much to lose to enter into a relationship. It will not be easy for her to operate with a spirit of submission (humility). The right answer to this equation is not always getting married. It just may be for the two of you to leave each other alone. To find the solution, ask yourself the following questions using discernment:

- Does this person have a teachable spirit?
- Does this person have a humble heart?
- Has this person ever been abused?
- What happened that dissolved my last relationship?
- Why did I divorce?
- Where does God stand in my life?

Follow up the answers to those questions with these:

- Am I desiring marriage because I'm in love?
- Is it for money?
- Is it because the sex is good?
- Is it because of loneliness?
- Are you getting too old and are ready to settle down?
- Is she pregnant?
- Is it because she has your children?
- Is it because she wants to get married?
- Is it because he has stability (car, house, and money)?
- Is it because he's fine and strong?

NOTE: The **ONLY** answer that matters is your response to the first question. The rest are selfish, deceptive, and manipulating.

If it's not love and not based on the Word, you may quickly fall into the traps of the enemy in the spiritual, physical, and financial areas of your life and marriage.

Men, remember that marrying a woman who has been in control of her home for a long time or has held a position of authority may require a lot of patience as God does what He has to do in both of you. Know that He will not change one without changing the other. Still, with a woman of this caliber, there is much love, respect, and sensitivity in her as well as class, style, and beauty. The most challenging aspect of the relationship will be determining if she will be willing to share her life with **YOU**. The only way to do that is to take your relationship before the Lord in prayer and let Him show you through His Word and by His Word the way to each other's heart so that you may have a blessed and prosperous marriage. God knows exactly how long and what it will take to bring both of you together and on one accord.

I'm going to pause here and pray that Christian pastors, leaders, and churches will stop participating in any type of dating service on the web or in newspapers. The website is exactly what it says it is: a web of entanglement. They open the door for the weak **AND** the strong to jump in the driver's seat and go for a test drive. Be careful, as there are many Christians involved in fornication and adultery using those avenues. They may be saved, but not necessarily delivered.

I Once Was Blind, But Now I See

Please don't give others a reason to go back to a life of sin, for the wages of sin is death.

Please don't give God a reason to call them home early — or maybe He will call **YOU** home first. You are your brother's keeper.

Please don't give Satan an open doorway into their lives.

Please don't "play" God. Let the Father choose for them by revealing to them what's really in their heart, not a questionnaire that reads well and that they can lie on.

REMEMBER: The Holy Spirit will lead you to all truth, not words of enticement.

Pastors, remember God is holding you responsible. Don't send them out to be devoured by the wolves. Don't be a pastor who helps Satan scatter the sheep. Don't have their blood on your hands. Don't lean on your own understanding or be wise in your own eyes.

Minister Aaron Weaver

A Prayer of Leadership

Father, in the Name of Jesus:

 I take authority over the spirit of Jezebel and Ahab. In Your Name, I release the spirits of witchcraft, controlling spirits, and passive spirits. In the Name of Jesus, I loose the spirit of leadership and God's love to the husband, the spirits of honor and respect for the husband to the wife, and the spirit of obedience to the children with a servant's heart to all of us.

 I bring this care before You, Lord, that you may do that which is needed in us, for Your Word says that we can cast our cares upon You, for You care for us.

In Jesus' Name,

Amen.

CHAPTER 7

SUBMISSION AND REBELLION

The Word of God says that rebellion is as the spirit of witchcraft (see 1 Samuel 15:23). At some point, everyone has been infected with that spirit because it came through the bloodline of man through Adam.

Men, in many instances, you will find a woman who has been brainwashed by a loudmouth, know-it-all friend or family member who has sown bad advice into her. Those people try to run her life, in the same manner, they have **RUINED** their own. Some women apply to their lives what they've seen or heard on soap operas and talk shows. The advice received may sound something like this:

- "Child, you don't need him. Kick him out!"
- "So what if you don't love him. Just get his money."
- "Girl, get a man who's married. When you're done with him, send him back home to his wife."
- "Give him some and hook him. Then, you will have him right where you want him!"
- "Get yourself a Sugar Daddy."
- "So what if you're pregnant! Just tell your husband the baby is his."
- "If he wants some sex, make him pay for it."
- "Honey, all men are dogs."
- "Say you were drunk and didn't remember what happened."
- "Obey??? Girl, you are NOT a dog!"
- "You're grown. You don't have to listen to him."

As heartbreaking as it is, this is another area where a third-party person gives unwise counsel to you in your relationship or marriage.

Some women feel they would rather stay single so that they can remain in control. Ladies, why would you speak a curse on yourself by saying, *"There are no more good men to be found"*? What happens when you put that out in the atmosphere is you will always find yourself with a no-good man (read Proverbs 18:21). Stop freely giving yourself away to those no-good men so that they can learn how to be the good man you're seeking. The more you sleep with those no-good men, the more you keep taking care of them, giving them no reason to get their life in order.

> **REMEMBER:** Two no-good people will never have a good relationship or marriage.

Men, if you want a good woman, you must first be a good man. You must walk, talk, dress, speak (without cussing), and most of all, carry yourself with respect, dignity, and integrity. These are God's standards you should have in place for yourself and things that must be developed in your upbringing. You must make these things a part of your lifestyle with everyone you encounter. If you are without these attributes, go back to the basics. Renew your mind and rededicate your life back to God. Ask Him to restore good and godly morals into your life. Depend on Him to make the change in your spirit-man and personal life. Most of all, let God guide you to the woman He has for you.

Ladies, let the Holy Spirit be your decision-maker. He will **NEVER** give you the following advice:

- *"Girl, if that were me, I'd make him pay!"*
- *"Let's follow him and see where he's going."*

- ➤ *"He's lying, girl. He has someone on the side. Get yourself someone on the side, too!"*
- ➤ *"You need to kick him out like I did with my last two husbands and three boyfriends."*
- ➤ *"Take your baby and leave!"*
- ➤ *"You need to make him pay for every time he made you cry."*

Ladies, to submit to your husband is to submit to him as the head of the house, Jesus as the Head over him, and God over us all (see 1 Corinthians 11:3).

But wait, men: Submitting goes both ways. How can you expect your wife or children to submit if you're not doing the same thing toward God? In the marriage vow, the words *"To love, honor, and obey"* intimidate and bring fear into the life of the wife. Ladies, remember that when you honor and obey your husband, you are honoring the Christ in him.

Now, if either of you asks the other to do something outside of the will of God or try to intimidate, control, or otherwise operate under a spirit of witchcraft or pride, then you have removed God from the marriage. In other words, a spirit of witchcraft does not apply to just potions and spells; it also includes manipulation, intimidation, controlling behaviors, deception, hypnosis, operating under a seducing spirit, and more.

Take a moment to read Galatians 5:19-20 to learn about the Fruit of the Spirit.

God will not accept anything that is not righteous in His sight. He will not accept anything with a hidden purpose or for selfish gain.

Look at what happened to Abram (Abraham): God did not tell him to take Hagar as a wife. God told him that Sarai (Sarah) would bear his child, but he listened to the voice of Sarai and made her bondmaid his wife. That was not God's will. God never said He would bring forth the promised child through the bondmaid, so He could not honor the union. If He did, He would be compromising (read Genesis 16:1-4). In the 4th and 5th verses, Sarai is sorry and deeply grieved. Further along in scripture, God told Abraham that the chosen child would be Isaac (read Genesis 17:19-21 to learn more).

The moral of the story is this: When you choose to do things on your own, you bring sin into the camp (house) as well as the marriage.

Examine yourself. How well did you listen to your parents, teachers, or others in positions of authority? If you chose to have everything go your way and only your way, then you can expect your child to be affected in a greater magnitude. Furthermore, if you don't take the time to deal with any anger you are harboring, you have set yourself up to fail and be bombarded by attack after attack by Satan's army.

Abusive Relationships

God does not want **ANYONE** to stay in an abusive relationship or marriage.

There are quite a few religions and people (even family members) that will tell people to stay in an abusive relationship or marriage. It is likely in response to them having been in one of their own, and their lives are filled with misery.

There is an untruth that says, *"You will go to Hell if you get a divorce."* It's also untrue that if you marry again after a divorce, you will be committing adultery because the "until death do we part" of the marriage vow means what it says.

REMEMBER: We are under grace now, not the law of sin and death.

Rebellion 101

Ladies, remember that when you are rebellious against your husband, it's like poking holes in your protective covering from demonic attacks. Your yelling, name-calling, and pinpointing what he's doing wrong does not help; it only causes more damage by inflicting your marriage with other spirits of destruction. You must use humility, wisdom, and the Word of God, for your weapons are not carnal but mighty through God in pulling down strongholds.

Men, have you ever known Jesus to hit or abuse anyone? **NO!** He took authority over all things while operating in the love, will, and purpose of God. We must represent Jesus, our Lord and Savior. We must be a good role model. I repeat: We are made in the image and likeness of God (see Genesis 1:26-27). We must first give respect to gain respect. Remember always that you are responsible for everything that happens in your home, relationships, and marriage. In other words, you are responsible for what goes on with your family as it pertains to keeping things in order or addressing things when they are out of order.

To the men: Following are seven levels we must learn to submit to in our lives.

1. Seek first the Kingdom of God and His righteousness (read Matthew 6:33).
2. Study to show yourself approved, rightly dividing the Word of Truth (see 2 Timothy 1:5).
3. Communication: First with God, and then getting to know that special woman in your life. Remember to ask a lot of questions about her. Meet her family and friends. Learn about their lifestyle. Be mindful that no matter how much you think you know, there is always more to learn.
4. Stay in prayer and in the Word. Continue to talk to each other even more after you're married. The reason for this is because many deep-rooted issues within both of you need to come to the surface.
5. Don't deny your spouse sex because you feel she doesn't "deserve it" or because you're trying to teach them a lesson. I don't dare consider that you're saving yourself for someone else outside of your marriage… Don't give the enemy a seat in your marriage. If sex between the two of you isn't satisfying or you're not having sex at all, take it to God first to get wise counsel and then your mate. In the same breath and opposite end of the spectrum, don't go overboard. Too much sex can be just

as bad as not getting enough. Remember that your body belongs to your spouse; don't abuse yourself.

6. Financial matters: This is a huge hurdle to overcome. Just because you have money doesn't mean you will be happy all throughout your marriage. The enemy (Satan) and his demonic forces will be on standby, waiting for an opportunity to come in and steal the money by trying to get you to use it in ungodly ways. Some examples of ungodly ways include:
   a. Buying drugs; gambling
   b. Watching or participating in pornography
   c. Frequenting a prostitute
   d. Calling perverted phone numbers
   e. Dialing any type of soothsayer
   f. Non-sufficient fund fees
   g. Payday loans
   h. Purchasing movies (DVDs) with cussing and perverted scenes
   i. Being told you don't have to support your church by tithing, so you don't

Stop listening to the lies of the enemy. Go to God in prayer and ask the Holy Spirit to guide you. Read His Word and learn His truths.

Be a good steward. Are you guilty of any of the following?
   a. Do you throw your clothes and shoes just anywhere when you remove them?
   b. Do you place them on the hanger any kind of way?
   c. Do you keep your house clean?

d. Do you let your children jump and climb on your furniture?
e. How well do you take care of the things that were given to you by others?

If you're guilty of abusing and misusing God's blessings, repent and gain a sincere appreciation for His gifts.

7. Do you believe the lie that bad credit is better than no credit? If so, don't believe it! It is a set up by the devil and the system. This lie will keep you in poverty, lack, and financial hardship with high interest, exorbitant payments, and less money in your pocket. What happens then? Foreclosure. Repossession. Bankruptcy. Are those what you really want?

Get rid of the junk. Clean up your house. Don't ask God to bless you with more or something better until you do.

New Level, New Devils

No matter who you are, you will always suffer persecution—especially as you draw closer to God. The closer you get to Him, the more you and your family will be attacked. If you have not accepted Jesus as your personal Lord and Savior yet, Satan already has you in his grasp.

Why is it in our nature to speak death more than life into our situations? A great deal of the time, we say negative things about people or situations because it's easy to speak negatively about the world before we see the good in it or the good that God is doing. With the media's influence, we often fail to recognize the hand of God moving.

REMEMBER: The more negatively you speak, the more evil will reign in your life.

Try this: Change your conversation. You will soon see a change in your life as well as in the world.

Negative talk is the result of a lifestyle of a person who has never been sure of himself/herself. They have never learned how to express themselves or keep company with others who think and speak the same way. These spirits can cause your prayers to go unanswered or delay your breakthrough.

REMEMBER: God **SPOKE** everything into existence. He gave Adam the same authority, which was also passed down to us.

A Prayer of Submission

My Heavenly Father:

Forgive me for not realizing the importance of submitting to my parents or persons in authority. Restore me, Dear God, that my family and I may be delivered from these spirits.

Also, Dear God, forgive me for not taking care of the possessions You have given me, including the money, gifts, and other things that my family and friends have sown into my life.

Father, take away the spirit of rebellion, selfishness, and pride in my life. Deliver me from the spirit of borrowing, poverty, and lack,

Humble me, O Lord, with a submissive spirit, that I may serve You and help others. Help me to choose my words carefully and not take part in negative talk.

In Jesus' Name,

Amen.

CHAPTER 8

THE YOUTH DILEMMA: PART 1

I Once Was Blind, But Now I See

I'm speaking directly to our youth here…

Some people will say that you're our future. Well, that's not exactly true. You are your **own** future first. The present is the beginning of your future. It's what you make of it and what you plan to do for yourself and future family.

On the other hand, you are our future when you keep your family name alive, for your name is what you inherited from your father. If you don't give your children your name, then your heritage will die.

If you choose to end your unborn child's life by abortion, then you have liquidated your future and the blessing of God that was passed down to you and your children. You are our future because you will be among those who supply the needs of both old and new generations.

One of the things that God hates is the shedding of innocent blood. If you don't want to raise your child, give him/her up to another family member. At least that child will still know who their family is. If you choose to give him/her up for adoption, at least there is someone who can give and show them love. Still, the **BEST** thing you can do is take responsibility and raise them yourself. God will provide you and your child with all the love you will need.

Young ladies, don't allow yourself to be persuaded into having sex, taking drugs, or getting drunk. This can lead to one or more boys (or men) having their way with you all night long. Don't multiply your sorrow by sleeping around and looking for love in all the wrong places.

Young men, when you respect young ladies, you're also respecting yourself, your mother, and future daughter as well. The same respect you show is the same that some boy (or man) will give your daughter and the same respect some girl (or woman) will give your son. This is the beginning of your journey into the gateway to manhood.

REMEMBER: Do not lean to your own understanding (Proverbs 3:5). Be not wise in your own eyes (Proverbs 3:7). If either of those scriptures applies to you, then you are operating in a state of immaturity.

However, as men, we play an important part in your future. It is our responsibility to give you good, wise counsel and godly advice and to help you make the right decisions in life. We are to pray that God always puts the right person in your path to guide you in the direction He wants you to do.

Think About It "Nugget": Young men, your grandparents worked to provide Social Security for your parents. Your parents work to provide Social Security for you. I ask you: Are you working to provide some type of security for you and your future family?

The Doggish Dilemma

In today's age, many men are operating under what people call a "doggish spirit." By nature, a dog is selfish and inconsiderate; they have no respect for anything or anyone else (without training).

I Once Was Blind, But Now I See

Women and girls refer to men as "dogs," but if they are sleeping with a different man every time, then they're operating as a female dog with a doggish spirit. Know that a male dog will sleep with **ANY** female dog if she lets him.

Are you willing to let this happen to you?

Ladies, don't let the enemy disrespect or degrade you this way.

Hollywood, beauty pageants, sex magazines, and strip clubs have no respect for you. Our government officials, the school system, and some parents have lost sight of their morals and self-respect.

REMEMBER: You get what you speak! If you continue to call yourself a b***h, then you will begin to act in that manner. No matter how you use the word, it's still self-degradation.

Do not let anyone cause you to lower yourself to that standard of living because you are being a tramp or slut.

- **Tramp:** A woman (or girl) who is sexually promiscuous.
- **Slut:** A woman (or girl) who is sexually promiscuous, especially a prostitute; a dirty, untidy woman.

The next young man or man you meet could be the one you fall hopelessly in love with. Do you really want to be presented to him and enter his life with either of those labels? Consider this: Will he be willing to forget your past? Will he support you as God heals you?

Young men, the same applies to you. The more you sleep around, the less likely you will be able to perform when you are ready to settle down.

If you have been raped or sexually abused…if you have been forced into or got involved with a same-sex person and feel that you can't get out…if you think that nobody will want you because of what you've been through…if you feel that you are now damaged goods, remember: God loves you and can help you turn your life around. Please don't give up on yourself because God hasn't given up on you.

If either of you are having sex or have children from more than one person, then both of you are operating under a seducing spirit. The man may have a Succubus spirit attached to him, and the woman, an Incubus spirit attached to her. These seducing spirits will cause you to lust after any man or woman, no matter their age. The desire for sex could be so strong, the spirits will have sex with you in your dreams.

REMEMBER: You are in the spirit world when you're asleep.

If the demon wasn't transferred to you by your parents, then there's a good chance it was assigned to you by one of your sex partners.

In the Bible, there was a prostitute called Mary Magdalene. Jesus cast out seven sexual devils from her (read Mark 16:19).

Young men, don't sell the girls short. There are male prostitutes as well, and they are called "gigolos."

I Once Was Blind, But Now I See

Whether male or female, don't give in to a promiscuous lifestyle. Some common excuses for succumbing include:

- *"Don't judge me."*
- *"You're not in my shoes."*
- *"If your dad would send me some money…"*
- *"I'm tired of not having…"*
- *"I'm tired of struggling."*
- *"It pays the bills."*
- *"It puts food on the table."*
- *"I did what I had to do to get…"*

You don't have to concern yourself with someone else judging you because you just judged yourself with your own words and actions.

As Christians, we can't judge a person, but we can judge the fruit they produce. Just remember that God and **ONLY** God can and will judge everyone on Judgment Day. God has said He would supply all that you need and has already given you a way to escape out of the mess. Leave that lifestyle alone (read Matthew 6:25-33). God gave you the power to get wealth, but not like that! Let God help you get your respect back.

If you're wrapped up in the money you're making, believe me when I say: You cannot take it with you to Heaven or Hell. There's nothing wrong with being rich, but when you let money rule you and all you're interested in is making **MORE** money, you have forgotten God, fallen away from Him, and fell into the love of money (read 1 Timothy 6:7-11). Don't let money give you false hope or enslave you. Scripture asks,

"What does it profit a man to gain the world and lose his soul?" (Matthew 12:19-20). Don't let money rule you; you must rule it!

If that classifies your life, ask God to forgive you, repent, and leave that lifestyle alone. Enter into God's Kingdom alive and well to reside in a mansion in Heaven explicitly designed for you.

Ladies, if you want the right type of man (not a doggish one or a pimp), the first thing you should do is give yourself respect and demand it from the person you're with, to include those you spend time with on and off the job.

Men, if you want a decent woman, then you should live as a man of God with respect for yourself and all women. Don't partake in cussing, drinking, smoking, vulgar music, and pornography. The more you entertain those spirits, the better your chances are of failure showing up in your life.

Lawmen of the Old West (sometimes called Sheriffs or Marshals) were used to go after those who have done an injustice to others. The would often deputize a group of men to form a posse.

God Almighty already has a posse, and they are called **INTERCESSORS**. These mighty prayer warriors gather together to pray (do warfare) on your behalf as well as for your family and the world. They are on call 24 hours a day to take back what the enemy has stolen from you. However, through your salvation, you can help others become saved, to include your children, their future children, family members, and friends. You can also help to keep many of them from going to

I Once Was Blind, But Now I See

Hell and the Lake of Fire, where all who oppose God will be cast into on Judgment Day.

REMEMBER: Once you have accepted Jesus as your Savior, you are responsible for sharing the Word and telling others about our Lord and Savior, Jesus the Christ.

There's no such thing as peer pressure that's holding you back. Peer pressure comes from those who get angry with you because you choose to be different. They don't understand you, so they attack. Be ever-mindful that the Word of God says you will be persecuted for your beliefs. Be strong enough, bold enough, and wise enough to let the Holy Spirit help you draw them into the light. Don't let them pull you back into the darkness.

Expect to initially be suddenly stricken with pride, low self-esteem, and fear. You may find yourself afraid to speak to your family, schoolmates, and even your girlfriend or boyfriend about your salvation because they may call you a "Jesus Freak." No one wants to be rejected by family and friends but remember this: If they can't receive you for who you are, then they were never your friends to begin with. Show them who you really are: a Christian—a child of God! If you're ashamed to honor Jesus before man, He will be ashamed to know you before God.

REMEMBER: It doesn't matter what others believe, say, think, or feel. Pride comes before a great fall, so don't fall for the enemy's slick tricks to discourage you from standing up boldly for Jesus.

So, what can cause an early death for our youth?

1. Cussing at your parents and other people, including those in authority. Participating in ungodly conversations at school, work, on the phone, or at home. Exodus 20:12 says, *"Honor thy father and mother, for this is the first commandment with a promise of long life."*
2. Listening to and singing songs that contain vulgar language talking about sex, murder, and hatred. These songs will affect the way you think, your spirit, your conduct, physical appearance, mental growth, and level of maturity. It will become so common, you will begin to think it's normal. This also includes movies with a lot of vulgar language and sex as well as horror movies, video games, and cartoons with very graphic scenes. If these things don't bother you, that means you have already fallen under the influence of these spirits.
    a. Example: If you're a smoker and in the midst of those who smoke, the smoking doesn't bother you. For those of us who don't smoke, it's very offensive, and sometimes it makes it difficult for us to breathe.

Don't let the things of the world cause you to lose your morals. They will endanger your soul and lead you down the path to Hell.

3. Maybe it's because some parents were never taught how to pray. As a result, you don't know how and cannot teach your children how to pray.
4. Maybe you know how to pray but are not praying with or teaching your children. Perhaps you're not praying for them in the right way, or you're not praying for them

at all. This leaves the doors open for the enemy to enter into their lives. Many of your adversities come from your bad decisions. They are not your parents' fault.

Take this test: Point just your pointer finger at something. The average person has three fingers pointing back at them. This means whatever you do to someone else that's not good will come back to you three times greater.

This concept can be applied to when you use profanity or are involved in a vulgar conversation. Whatever you speak in the conversation will come back to you…but with more intensity and can affect your family, home, money, sexual relationship in your marriage, job performance, and bring forth an early death. The devil can now use the curse in any way he chooses.

In the Book of Deuteronomy 28:1-15, it tells about the blessing for obedience. Beginning in verse 16, it speaks of the curses that are a result of sin. The curses still apply to us today through our sins, for God cannot let sin go unpunished. However, because of the birth, death, and resurrection of our Lord Jesus the Christ, we are not under the Law any longer, but rather we are covered by grace.

Jesus died so that all of our sins can be forgiven, but our sins still have consequences. What a blessing we have in the Advocate, which is now our Savior, Jesus Christ!

Chapter 9

The Youth Dilemma: Part 2

I Once Was Blind, But Now I See

Personal Encounter

Let me share a part of my life story with you that very few people know:

My parents divorced when I was about a year old. I very seldom saw my father after that. He would sometimes call on holidays, and we would see him in the Summer. I knew very little about him, but the little I did know, I keep as a memory. I was about 18 years old when my brother was killed at the age of nineteen. My father died about three years after my brother's death.

I felt alone, hurt, and angry. There was no man I knew who I thought would understand the sudden burst of anger and loss I experienced. With both of them out of my life, I had to be the man of the house—a role I was not mentally prepared for. The spirit of anger rose up inside of me.

From the age of 18 until 25, I did just about everything but die (and actually came close to doing that several times). On two occasions, I was almost electrocuted; on two other occasions, I nearly drowned.

I was well-known in Mississippi and Hartford, Connecticut (not necessarily in a postive way).

When I reached the age of 25, God sent a young lady into my life as a friend. She showed me that according to the Word of God, I must be born again and accept Jesus as my Lord and personal Savior in order to be saved. I was already saved but needed to rededicate my life back to Christ. After talking to her,

I did just that. At the time, I was shacking up with my girlfriend. That same night, I left my girlfriend but soon fell back into my old lifestyle.

During this time, I learned a little Karate and Kung Fu and went to wrestling matches. None of those things filled the void in my life. The only things that gave me peace and pleasure were reading my Bible, listening to gospel music, and watching Christian movies on television and at the theater.

Your Misery Will Become Your Ministry

Today, my job is to minister to men, women, and the youth. My message is that what they're doing is not worth it and to turn their lives around before it's too late.

I spent at least 15 to 20 years of my life involved with women who were married or engaged to be married. God tugged on my heart, and I realized I was playing the fool, just like many of you reading this are doing today.

Before my change of heart, I never viewed my indiscretions in that manner. I always thought that if I liked her and we cared for each other, it was okay! I was justifying my actions while denying the truth. *"By thy words, thou shall be justified, and by thy words, thou shall be condemned."* Read Matthew 12:33-37. Those words set **ME** straight!

Change of Heart

In 1992, I met Verda, but she was engaged. Immediately, I did not want to get involved; however, her engagement was a strange one. God began His work in us on our first date. He showed me His love and the heart of her as well. God quickened my heart and changed it. He asked me, *"Do you want her for your wife?"* I replied, *"Yes, God: I do!"* He then instructed me to be patient and continued to draw us closer together.

He gave me a vision of a wedding ring on my finger. Even then, God was doing a new thing in me. That same year, I joined her church. The Lord told the pastor that He would speak to everyone that day. I listened closely, but all I heard was two words: *"Be strong."* I was a little disappointed at first because everyone else at the church was receiving lengthy downloads from the Lord.

About a month later, during the men's ministry, one of the brothers was reading scripture and the fullness of the *"Be strong"* message hit me. At the time the words were spoken, *"Be strong"* was all I needed. In that meeting, the Lord was ready to give me more of what He had to say, which was a message from Joshua 1:7-9:

"Only be thou strong and very courageous, turning not to the right hand or to the left that you may prosper wherever you go. This book of the law shall not depart out of thy mouth; but thou shall meditate therein day and night. Remember: Do not despise small beginnings, and little becomes much when given to the LORD. [There were times when doubt and fear came upon me. I was like a fish out of water, and this lifestyle was one I was very unfamiliar with.] Have I not commanded thee? Be strong and of good courage; be not afraid, neither be thou dismayed: for the Lord thy God is with thee."

I studied that passage of scripture for quite some time as I began to learn of God and know Him in more of an intimate way. They were the scriptures God gave me to study. This was the starting point of my new life and walk with God.

In 1993, God told me these words:

"Everything you know about being a man you must forget. It doesn't apply here. You must become a man of God and put away the ways of the world."

Everything I knew for the past 43 years was of no further use to me anymore.

God had already shown Verda that I had a childlike heart. She and I continued to talk and spend time together. After a year and a half, we began to experience some issues in our relationship, which brought back bad memories. I didn't realize that God was peeling away those things by bringing them to the surface. The issues brought us to the point where we had to back up for a while. That was when God gave me Matthew 6:33:

"But seek ye first the Kingdom of God and His righteousness…"

The reason for this was because I was too focused on Verda and not our Heavenly Father.

REMEMBER: God is a jealous God. We shall not have any other god before Him (see Exodus 20:3).

I Once Was Blind, But Now I See

On March 18, 1995, at 12:00 noon, we married. Verda had been celibate for nine years when we met and for three years after we met, which made 12 years for her. I was celibate for the three years we knew each other before getting married. God did it for us, and He can do it for you, too! It's not too late to make a change in your life.

In 1997, God gave me the revelation of what He meant, and this is what He said:

"Aaron, you had to become as a little child so I could develop you and bring you up to the level I need you to be."

When you let **GOD** do it, it will be done on time and in the right way. God is first in my life and also the center of it.

Make the Change

Don't waste your fruitful and youthful years. Remember that whatever you give up for Christ will last (read Philippians 3 in its entirety). Our reality is the spirit realm; it is eternal. Our lives and everything on this earth are only temporary. Our bodies are just a place for our spirits to reside. Our homes, cars, jobs, money, clothes, and other things we use on this earth will be left behind when we die. Enjoy them while you live; don't live to enjoy them.

Remember that it's up to you and only you to choose your destiny. The path you take in life can be altered by the choices you make.

- Will you use drugs…or not?
- Will you sleep around…or not?
- Will you be abusive to your mate…or not?
- Will you disrespect your parents…or not?
- Will you sleep with a married man/woman or a same-sex partner…or not?
- Will you abort that baby…or not?

For example, if someone tells you they're going on a trip or to a friend's or relative's house and someone terminates their life intentionally while en route, that is an act of murder. The same applies to a pregnant woman. If she, the doctor, or clinic terminates the life of that baby, that is an act of premeditated murder.

The decisions are yours to make. The choice is up to you to make the right one. Choose life! Choose Christ! (Read Proverbs 18:20-21.)

Please remember that your spirit is the very essence of God. We began in the mind of God (see Genesis 2:27; 5:2). God knew you before you were in your mother's womb. The manifestation of life began when you were conceived (just as it was with Mary, the mother of Jesus, when she agreed to receive God's gift of salvation for her and the whole world).

From the time a woman learns that she's pregnant, she doesn't go around saying that she's going to have a fetus. She says, *"I am going to have a baby."*

A fetus is the life of a baby, just like a baby is the life of a toddler; a toddler is the life of a teenager, and a teenager is the life of a man or woman. A man or woman is the life of an older adult, and an older adult is the remaining life before death. Death is the doorway leading to where you will spend eternity. Will it be spent in the New Heaven or the Lake of Fire? It all depends on you! Will you accept Jesus Christ as your Savior?

NOTE: For those of you who haven't seen or don't know who your birth parents are, if you happen to one day meet them, don't be harsh towards them. Just say, *"Mom/Dad, I thank God that you didn't abort me."* No matter the reason for their absence, please forgive them.

More importantly, don't forget to forgive yourself.

Bad Decisions: The Doorway to Your Dilemma

Some of you reading this may have already accepted Jesus as your Savior, but because of your friends or other negative influences, you choose to walk in an unholy lifestyle. No matter the reason, I can assure you it's not a good one. Friends are good to have but going along with something or doing something just to be accepted is unwise.

Your foolish decisions were what got you into whatever predicament you are in now, such as having a hatred for someone because of the color of their skin or beating up someone for not having your $5.00 when you asked for it are examples of foolishness (read Leviticus 19:17-18). Nothing has been proven except that you know how to be Satan's fool. Stop operating under the stupid, gullible, or controlling spirit!

Your spirit knows what is right but will still do what it wants to do, even if it's wrong. Wrong decisions are stupid, pointless, and senseless. I'm not calling **YOU** stupid; I'm addressing the spirit under which you're operating. Be sure you do the same.

Masturbation

Masturbation is known by many names, to include "Choking the Chicken" and "Spilling the Seed." God is very displeased with this act and has actually slew men for doing it (read Genesis 38:7-8).

When you use a condom, you are also spilling (wasting) the seed by catching it and throwing it away. That is a form or murder and abortion, for your sperm is alive, and you are killing millions of children at one time by tossing them in the trash. As such, the blame for that act of murder cannot be blamed on just the woman, doctor, or clinic. Those children's blood is on **YOUR** hands.

Now that you **KNOW** masturbation is a sin, stop the killing!

The Blame Game

Far too often, I hear comments about what "the white man" is doing to you and what they have done to our ancestors. Yes, it's true that they killed, raped, and hung our people from trees, but at the same time, you are killing the black man, woman, and children with drugs, alcohol, abortions, smoking cigarettes or marijuana (which cuts off the oxygen supply to your brain), guns, and gang violence.

If you're pregnant or have children, you must make a change in your lifestyle. If you live in the "ghetto," change your mindset and stop wanting to live on government assistance for the rest of your life. Make a conscious choice to live in a better environment for you and your children. Begin to think more highly of yourself. Become a better person. Get it together and move away from that environment. You can do it, and God will help you if you ask Him!

REMEMBER: The government and its political cronies are centered on destroying our people by making it easier for you to destroy yourself. Will you give them the satisfaction of letting them know you don't care about yourself and family?

Living on the system and having babies knowing that the government will take care of you and the children for a lifetime is unwise. Making it plain, all you are doing is living in prison—with the White House and Congress as the wardens. So, now you have introduced your children and future generations to a life of poverty and lack.

Listen: If you think having children and living together makes you a family, then you are sadly mistaken. When a man and woman get married and children are involved, **THAT** constitutes a family. If you're not legally married (according to what *GOD'S* Word says), then you are just a man and woman living together. Stop listening to man when they say that after six months, you are "common-law married." God did not ordain this lifestyle from the beginning, and He does not condone (overlook) it now. If you choose to continue living in sin, be prepared to receive God's judgment.

Lastly, you need to stop feeding off of anger and an unforgiving spirit. God is a God of recompense and vengeance. He will repay those who do evil in His sight.

REMEMBER: God has already forgiven you; now, you must forgive yourself, forgive them, and move on.

A Selfish Dilemma

Let's start this section with a common scenario in today's society:

You are a drug dealer who makes close to $10,000 a week. You have a wife, three children, a luxurious home, and two expensive cars. You think you have "arrived" — until you are killed in the street, or you get caught and go to jail. The judge sentences you to 15-25 years…no bail. What do you suppose is going to happen to your family in your absence?

Well, maybe your wife will get another man (if she didn't already have one on the side). She begins using the drugs you used to sell. Maybe the children will get a hold of the drugs, overdose, and die.

The downward spiral doesn't end there!

Your wife may have to sell the home and cars. The children are taken away and placed in the foster care system.

Their mother is either dead, homeless or enters a life of prostitution to support her drug habit.

Ask yourself: What have you given your family? The answer is: Nothing but a wasted life.

This is an example of a poor excuse for a so-called man because he chose to give his family a life of poverty, imprisonment, and death. The same applies to a woman who does the same thing, by the way.

Stop listening to the enemy's lies. Ask God for guidance. Walk away from that selfish lifestyle and put down the guns. Please don't expose your children to these evil deeds. Give everyone—including yourself—a chance to live and have a prosperous future.

Think about it like this: The only eyes you truly look good in are Satan's eyes. Everyone who comes along and pats you on the back while saying *"You're doing it big, man/woman!"* when you are in that type of lifestyle is under the devil's influence.

If you have a drug or alcohol problem, let God work it out. He knows how to get the job done. Cast your cares on Him, for He cares for you!

The Seductive Dilemma

Men, do you realize that when you wear your pants below your butt, you are advertising yourself to other men who have a desire to have sex with men? You are arousing the spirit that's attached to them to desire and lust after you, and God will hold you responsible for that enticement. Wearing your clothes in that manner is not only a perverted spirit, but it is also accompanied by a trifling spirit and a dysfunctional spirit. It is also an ignorant and immature spirit.

Ladies, the same thing applies to you! When you wear clothes that expose your body in a revealing way, you are not only causing men to lust after you but also women who desire you as well. You, too, will be held accountable for arousing lustful spirits.

REMEMBER: The clothing industry doesn't care about you. You're the one walking around looking like a clown, prostitute, slut, or looking as if you're carrying a load of poop in your pants!

After Death Comes Judgment

Let's get one thing clear: Those of us who are saved and will be in the Kingdom of God with Jesus and the rest of the saints, our deeds will be judged by fire. They will be tried by the Fire of Righteousness, which is the Fire of Truth and Love. Every single thing you've ever done will pass through this Fire. If it doesn't get consumed by the Fire, then you will receive a reward. If it is consumed, you will still be saved but will have no reward.

During the tribulation, pure hell will be unleashed on the earth. Those who accept Jesus at that time will still be saved. This time will be the world's second chance for eternal life; however, when the second trumpet sounds, those who have not accepted Christ as their Savior or those who have received the mark of the Beast will be doomed to spend eternity in the Lake of Fire with Satan, his angels, and the Beast.

Don't let this unfortunate situation be your future or that of your family. Change your ways and accept Jesus as your Savior before it's too late. If you have not repented of your sins and not accepted Jesus as your Savior, I encourage you to do so NOW. Please don't forget to pray for your family.

REMEMBER: The rest of this very day or tomorrow is not promised to you.

No one — and I mean **NO ONE** — is worth you losing out on Jesus and eternal life; not your wife, husband, son, daughter, mother, father, government, co-workers, pastor, or so-called friends. The choice is yours. What will you choose on this day: eternal life in Heaven or eternal life in Hell?

May God bless you as you learn from my shortcomings and mistakes. The lifestyle you're living is not worth eternal damnation of your soul.

A Prayer of Repentance

Dear God:

My life is a rollercoaster, full of ups and downs, curves and uncertainties. I ask You, O Lord, in the Name of Jesus, to deliver me from all the generational curses in my life and to give me a spirit of boldness and wisdom to stand up for You wherever I go and not be afraid of what my family and friends may think or say.

Lord, give me the wisdom to dress appropriately and to not be led by fads.

Dear God, renew my mind. Take away the desire to drink, smoke, and sell or use drugs. Deliver me from these spirits. Come into my heart and save me.

I accept You, Jesus, as my Lord and personal Savior. I rededicate my life to God today.

In Jesus' Name,

Amen.

CHAPTER 10

INSIGHT, DREAMS, AND VISIONS

Everyone has insight. If you've ever envisioned owning a car, buying a house, or working your dream job and made moves to obtain it, that is called "insight" — whether it comes to you in a vision or dream. Some people ignore them. The visions and dreams are revealed to you for a reason, whether you choose to pay attention to them or not.

It's the same way with God. He has given you the authority and power to see yourself as He does. God wants you to reach the level He already has ordained for you before the foundation of the world! The closer you get to Him and the more you study His Word, the greater your insight will be; however, be aware that the greater things grow, the enemy will find ways to attack you and your family. During this time, your faith will be tested. Don't give up; don't faint.

The Lord God Almighty had my wife, Verda, instill in me the following: *"Everything begins in the spirit realm first and then is manifested in the flesh [natural]."*

NOTE: Be careful. The enemy can also invade your dream and visions as well. You must bring them before God and THEN share them with your husband/wife or pastor.

The Cave

One night, while dreaming, I found myself in a meadow. It was filled with flowers and rich, green grass. As I looked across the field, I saw a large, black hole in the midst of the meadow.

I Once Was Blind, But Now I See

I could hear people crying, screaming, and yelling in pain. I knew then it was Hell. I cried out to God, *"Lord, I do NOT want to go there!"* Immediately after I said that, the hole disappeared.

Later that same night, I had the dream again. This time, I said, *"Lord, I'll go if You will go with me."*

Instantly, I was taken to one of the levels inside of Hell. On this level, it was as dark as a cave, but I was still able to see (it was like when the lights go out, and after a while, your eyes adjust a little to the darkness). I could hear moaning and yelling all around me. As I looked to my left, I saw figures of dead people walking up against the wall of the cave. They had chains on their hands and shackles on their feet. They looked just like skeletons and had a thin layer of green patches of skin covering their bones.

There was also a hairy beast that continuously struck them with a whip as they walked almost motionless through the darkness across from me.

I heard the voice of the Lord say, *"Look not to the right or left, but look straight ahead."* As I did, I could feel the beast watching me. I paid him no attention.

I was then led down a path to another level. There, I saw a pit covered with iron bars; however, a section of it had been removed. I saw a man come out of the opening of the pit. He was dressed in white and came to stand behind me.

When I looked to my right, I saw another beast in the likeness of a man, but this beast had two curved horns protruding from his head. As I looked at him, I saw he had hooves for feet. I then told him to give me the keys. I stretched out my hand, and the beast instructed another beast to surrender the keys to me. (I had no idea at the time what the keys were for or why I even asked for them.)

As I turned around to leave their presence, I was amazed to see that there were now four men dressed in white behind me, not just the one I saw earlier. I followed them out of Hell and back into the meadow. I turned back around just in time to see the hole closing up behind me. When I turned to follow the men in white, I saw one of them go into the church I was attending at the time. When I arrived, I was asked if I had the keys. I responded, "Yes, I do."

I was instructed by God to tell this dream in its entirety to my pastor.

The Meaning

The figures of those who were in chains and shackles are lost souls. They were in bondage and tormented by whatever sin they were being afflicted with.

When I received the keys, I heard the name "Gatekeeper"—the protector of a gateway to a person's life (to help keep out the enemy, evil spirits, demons, and even people who mean them no good or opt to give them unwise counsel).

I Once Was Blind, But Now I See

The four men in white were the Gospel: Matthew, Mark, Luke, and John.

I learned then that I am called into the ministry.

A Night to Remember

Another dream I had some time ago involved me walking in a dark place in the rain. I climbed a lot of stairs that seemed to be on the side of a building. There was a doorway I was supposed to go through to call out for someone, but there were electrical cables strung across the doorway. As I began to crawl under them, I was electrocuted.

The Revelation

That dark place was on the night shift at a shipyard where I was working at the time. My foreman told me to call someone. As I went up the gangplank on the side of the ship, I began to remember the dream.

When I reached the top of the ship, I saw the electrical cables strung across the doorway. I immediately turned around and went back downstairs. I shared my dream with the foreman. He looked at me strangely. I don't know what expression I had on my face, but he told me to sit down and not to worry; he would send someone else.

The Flame

In this dream, my wife and I were in Heaven dancing in the air over the Throne Room floor of God. I could see figures like angels standing at attention against the wall, but none of them were on the Throne Room floor.

When we finished dancing, we were both at the bottom of the stairs that led to God's Throne. I backed out with my head bowed down. As I exited the door, my wife hastily brought me a sword. When she placed it into my hand, it turned into a flaming sword.

The Meaning

The next night, one of the deacons of our church came over to visit me where I was working. I began talking to him about the dream. He looked at me with such amazement! He told the pastor and the other men there about my dream. That night, the Lord instructed the pastor to change the name of the men's ministry to "Flaming Swords."

Angels

Everyone, at some point in life, has had an encounter with an angel. However, more and more people dismiss it as if it never happened. Others choose not to say anything because they fear what people may think. Still, others choose not to believe it happened.

There are different types of angels:

- **Guardian Angels**—These are angels God has given charge (assignment or command) to watch over and protect us, but these angels cannot do their job if we don't put them to work.

- **Ministering Angels** — These are angels that talk to us, just as they did to Jesus when He was in the wilderness.
- **Archangels** — These are angels that war on our behalf. They are our military angels and fight on our behalf 24 hours a day, seven days a week. These angels have wings.

The Shoes

On one occasion, before Verda and I were married, we were having a conversation about a pair of shoes she was interested in buying. She could not find them anywhere. Later, she drove me to work at the Lake Forest Plaza in New Orleans.

As we sat in the parking lot of the Plaza, a lady walked up to her and asked, *"Do you know someone who can use some shoes?"*

Much to our surprise, she didn't have just one or two pairs; she had a large, black bag filled with different types of shoes — including the ones Verda had been looking for! To add icing to the cake, **THEY WERE BRAND NEW!**

When Verda turned around to thank the woman, she was nowhere to be seen (keep in mind that the parking lot was just about empty, and there were no other cars around us).

REMEMBER: Scripture reminds us to be careful how we entertain strangers, for they may be angels in disguise!

Sudden Impact

One foggy day, a friend of mine and I were on our way to work. We were running late, and I was driving very fast on the interstate. I didn't realize I was approaching my turn when suddenly, a white car flew across my path. I quickly turned my steering wheel to the right to avoid crashing into it.

To my surprise, if that car hadn't crossed in front of me, I'm sure I wouldn't be here today. In the fog, I didn't realize I was heading straight for the guardrail on the interstate — **AT FULL SPEED!**

After thanking God for His protection, I began to slow down. I was still able to see the white car in front of me because the fog started to lift in that area. When I turned to ask my friend if she was okay, she replied that she was. As I turned my focus back to the road, the white car had disappeared. Why is this amazing? Because it was at least a three-mile stretch before the next exit!

The Envelope

One time, our light bill, water bill, home phone bill, cell phone bill, and a bill for some products we ordered were all due at the same time. The total was roughly $650.00. I placed the money for the bills in a banking envelope.

When I arrived at my destination to pay the bills, I was about the 14th person in line. When I became the 5th person, a man tapped me on the shoulder, bent down in front of me with a smile on his face, and handed me the envelope that was by my feet. I looked down at the envelope and turned to thank him, but he was gone.

The envelope was identical to the one I entered with, so I thought I had somehow dropped it. Nope! **MY** envelope was still in my pocket!

I was puzzled because out of all the people in line in front of me, no one else saw it or picked it up. When I approached the window to pay the bills, to my surprise, the envelope handed to me by the man had exactly $650.00!

A Close One

This was another event that happened to me at the same shipyard where I worked.

I was repairing some pipe for the insulation department. I climbed up to the next level, which is between 10 – 18 feet over the set of pipes. All of a sudden, I slipped off a pipe and fell to the pipes below. Instead of falling in between them (where I would have gotten stuck), I fell and hit the outside pipe. After hitting the pipe, I suddenly bounced up while holding my side. It was as if I was yanked back up as soon as I hit the pipe below.

The initial diagnosis was that I had two broken ribs. When I went to get a second opinion, I learned I had **FOUR** broken ribs: one next to my heart, one next to my lungs, one next to my spleen, and one next to my kidney.

I believe that if my Guardian Angel had not pulled me up, I wouldn't be here today to tell you about the experience.

Why? Because the doctors could not explain how each of my broken ribs had a jagged edge yet did not pierce any of my vital organs.

The Dog

One day, I went with a friend to her mother's house to clean a refrigerator that her mom had given her.

Her mom had a red Doberman Pinscher in the backyard. She went outside to bring the dog into the house, however, after some time had passed, I heard a sound as if the back door had closed. After hearing that, I entered the yard. When I reached the halfway mark from the front to the backyard, the dog came from the back of the house. I was too far from the front gate and too close to the dog to make any sudden movement or even yell for help.

As I spoke softly and said, *"God, I put my trust in You,"* I felt an overshadowing peace cover me. The dog slowly walked up to me, and the Holy Spirit brought back to my memory to never stretch out your hand with your fingers extended. As the dog approached, I stretched out the back of my hand to the dog. To my surprise, the dog began licking the back of my hand and even stayed by my side as I cleaned the refrigerator.

After some time had passed, my friend came out the back door and screamed with amazement! She hysterically called her mother, and both of them said the dog had **NEVER** let a stranger in their yard before.

Miracles

Miracles happen every day. In many cases, people may be at the point of death, and by some unexplainable event, they are miraculously saved or rescued. In some instances, Ministering or Guardian Angels guide someone to help the person in distress.

Often, these angels resemble a person—a friend or family member, for instance—who has passed away. They may even look like someone who stays just down the street or hundreds of miles away. However, when they locate the person who helped them, the person is either confined to a bed, wheelchair, blind or has been in a coma for a long time. How did they know you were in trouble? Their spirit knew, and your angels were put on assignment! We can thank the Holy Spirit for intervening on someone's prayer for you or on God's command.

What Type of Light Are YOU?

Are you letting your light shine or have you dimmed your light? If you've dimmed your light, have you done so because of the company you keep? Maybe you choose to let it shine whenever you want to be "seen" as a Christian...

A Vision and Revelation

After writing the phrase above, I gave God thanks in prayer. I was led to put on my music and begin to pray in the Spirit. While doing so, I was sent to a place of total darkness. I had no idea why God put me in that place.

What I saw were dim images moving about in the darkness. I looked at myself and saw that I was brightly lit. As I progressed through the darkness, the images began to light up and approach me. To my surprise, those images were other Christians wandering in darkness. Their lights were so dim, they couldn't be exposed for who they really were.

Children of God, we are the light! That light also shines from within. We must keep our light shining so that those who are in darkness can be drawn to the Christ in other Christians and us as well.

They Are Not Dead

For years, after a loved one leaves this world, we say they died or that they are dead. The atypical response is, *"Sorry for your loss."* But they are **NOT** dead; neither did we lose them!

God stressed to me that when His children leave this world, they are not dead; they just went home to be with Him.

This is what Jesus was trying to tell His disciples when He said to them that Lazarus was asleep. They did not understand His message, and neither do many Christians today.

We don't die. We are a spirit. The shell of a body that we live in goes to sleep (see John 11:11-14), but our spirit remains awake and alive! The body goes back into the earth from where it came and takes the penalty of sin with it, which is death. The spirit goes back to the Lord.

Nothing that the **LORD** God has ever created or made is totally destroyed; it just changes form. A perfect example of this is how Lucifer went from being a beautiful angel to an evil being (although sometimes, he is referred to as "The Angel of Light").

Another example is when a forest, tree, or building is burned down. It is not completely destroyed; it just changes form. The residue of what it was is still there in ash form.

God dealt with me on this when my wife, Verda, went home to be with Him. He said, *"Don't say that she is dead because she is not. My Spirit lives in her, and I cannot die; neither can she."*

REMEMBER: Those who accept Jesus as their Savior will never die (read John 3:3-6; 16).

Jesus

It is March 28, 2009, at 9:43 in the evening. I began reading about the birth of Jesus in the Book of Matthew and also about how the wise men found Him in a house with his mother, Mary. I also read some reference scriptures regarding this event as well.

Afterward, the Lord began to reveal to me the different names and positions that Jesus functioned in from the time He was in Heaven, until His birth, and into His manhood.

In Heaven, Jesus was called "The Word." This is who He is, what He is, and always will be. When the Lord spoke to the Virgin Mary (in Matthew 1:23), He told her to call Jesus

Immanuel (meaning God is with us). This was His second spiritual name. As Jesus (meaning Savior) was being born, the first thing that showed was His crown (the crown of His head). Jesus fulfilled the prophecy of the King of Jews, the King of Kings, and the Lord of Lords being born.

Just the same, the crown of our head is shown so that we may also become kings, queens, princes, and princesses as we become sons and daughters of God.

So, Jesus was born and had His human name, which He used for about 30 years until He was baptized by John. After His baptism, the Holy Spirit descended and rested upon Him as a dove (representing the Holy Spirit). At that point, His two spiritual names (The Word and Immanuel) were joined together as one, crowning Him as Jesus (Savior) Christ (Messiah; The Anointed One).

So, you see: Jesus had two spiritual names and one human name. Not only did He have a human name with a purpose to fulfill, but He also had His spiritual name (Christ, The Anointed One) as well.

Jesus also had three levels of ministry He functioned in (some people call them "titles"):

1. The Son of God
2. The Son of Man
3. The Son of David

I Once Was Blind, But Now I See

A New Revelation

As I was meditating on the Word of God, He placed in my spirit a revelation concerning babies.

What He revealed to me was that when babies are born, the reason they cry is because they have been separated from Him (God Almighty), both spiritually and physically. The babies become a product of the world and will need a savior.

Babies also encounter fear as they enter into a world of sin, just as a person cries out in anguish, fear, and pain. They sense their separation from God in the same way Jesus felt His separation from the Father when He was on the cross, for God could not look upon sin. With that disconnect from our Heavenly Father, they have a sin nature. Why? Because it was passed down from the beginning through the bloodline of Adam: the first human sinner (see Genesis 2:17).

Scripture tells us that Cain slew his brother Abel and Abel's blood cried out to God from the earth. Jesus' innocent blood spilled on the earth as He was beaten and whipped as He made His way down that road to Calvary to be crucified. After His death, He was stabbed in His side with a spear (God hates the shedding of innocent blood).

Every innocent person whose blood was spilled or will be spilled in the future—whether by murder, abortion, witchcraft, or accident—must be redeemed with the innocent blood of Christ.

REMEMBER: Without the shedding of Christ's blood, there can be no redemption of sin.

I Once Was Blind, But Now I See

A Prayer of Trust

Dear God, in the Name of Jesus:

Let me not dismiss my dreams or visions but let me bring them before You in prayer that I may receive revelation knowledge and clarity of their meaning by Your Spirit, as well as what You would have me to do.

Father, strengthen me that I may trust in You, God, and not discard my visions and dreams because I feel they are unimportant. I realize now that they are not just for my benefit but for others as well.

Father, I must trust You in everything You do or give me in a dream, vision, or experience. I now know that it's for my good.

My Lord, My God: I thank You for trusting in me. Strengthen me with Your Spirit as I continue to trust in You.

In Jesus' Name,

Amen.

CONCLUSION

I Once Was Blind, But Now I See

Why Was This Book Written?

In 2004, while we were still living in New Orleans, Louisiana, my wife met a woman of God who was a prophet. I believe she was bringing over either some herbal or organic seasoning to the house for my wife.

The prophet spoke many things into our lives that day. Before she left, she spoke to me and said the Lord wanted me to write a book for men and to include my life's story and experiences—but it must **ALSO** contain the Word of God.

I pondered over this and asked myself, *"Who? ME? I don't know anything about writing, and my grammar is not the best."* With those things flowing through my mind, I realized I was already on my way upstairs to my computer. I sat down and stared endlessly at the blank screen. As I sat there looking hopelessly at the monitor, the phone rang. My wife answered and told me who it was. The voice on the other end said to me that God said to tell me to title the book *I Once Was Blind, But Now I See*.

I was going to start the first line of the body of this work with the word "men," but it came out "many." My fingers just started hitting keys, and the words began to flow. I had no idea what I was writing. After a while, the Holy Spirit stopped me and had me look at what was written. I didn't even have a title for the first chapter He had me write!

After about 25 pages, I wanted to stop and end the book, but I was pressed to continue writing.

For the next three pages, I jotted down what I wanted to say. After reading them, the pages that I chose to write made no sense. I wrote a few more pages, and they made no sense at all either. So, I deleted them. After doing that, the Lord spoke to me and said, *"Aaron, you must renew your mind."* That is how Chapter One got its title. In like manner, the rest of this book was given to me.

As time went on, the Lord gave my wife Psalm 45:1 because it spoke about the pen. I never really studied or read that passage before until this moment.

It is now September 30, 2014, and I **NOW** realize how much it related to this book. It is my sincerest prayer that something you've read has touched, inspired, and encouraged you to remove the blinders and **SEE**!

"My heart is inditing [stirring] a good matter:
I speak of the things which I have made touching the king:
my tongue is the pen of a ready writer."
Psalm 45:1

Closing Prayer – A New Beginning for You

In the Name of Jesus:

May this book open your eyes to the awesomeness of God and the greatness that's inside of you. May you take a stand for the Lord God and your family.

May the Lord draw you closer to Him than ever before. May the yearning for Him grow stronger each and every day. May God bless and prosper you in Him as He guides you through your life.

May we always remember to choose Christ, who is Eternal Life. Anything or anyone else is a false door to your salvation and the Kingdom of God.

REMEMBER: Choose Life; Choose Christ!

In Jesus' Name,

Amen.

Minister Aaron Weaver

www.ingramcontent.com/pod-product-compliance
Lightning Source LLC
Chambersburg PA
CBHW071913110526
44591CB00011B/1661